TEACHING METHODS AN

REMEDIAL SPELLING

Spelling Made *Easy* SERIES

Dictations to assess specific spelling difficulties in teenagers and adults

(For use with 'Put it Right')

by
Violet Brand

Published by **Brand**Books

England
www.Brandbooks.co.uk

Remedial Spelling
First published in 1985
Second impression 1987
Third impression 1988
Fourth impression 1990
Fifth impression 1991
Sixth impression 1991
Seventh impression 1992
Eighth impression 1993
Ninth impression 1994
Tenth impression 1995
Eleventh impression 1998
Twelfth impresion 1999
Thirteenth impression 2000
by Egon Publishers Ltd.

Original copyright © Egon Publishers Ltd
and Violet Brand,
ISBN 0 905858 32 8

Copyright assigned to BrandBooks
(a division of G & M Brand Publications Ltd)
and Violet Brand 2002

10 digit ISBN 1-904421-10-5
13 digit ISBN 978-1-904421-108

All rights reserved. No part of this book may be reproduced or transmitted in any form or by any means, electronic or mechanical, including recording or by any information storage or retrieval system without permission in writing from the publisher.

Contents

	Page
Guide to the use of Remedial Spelling	3
Teaching Method	5
Test passage 1 (short vowels)	9
Test passage 2 (ee, oo, or ar)	10
Test passage 3 (long vowel/silent e)	12
Test passage 4 (ai, oa, ir, ou)	14
Test passage 5 (ea, [ē], ay ur, aw)	16
Test passage 6 (oi, er, all, al, ea [ĕ])	18
Test passage 7 (ow, igh, a [ar], o [ŭ])	20
Test passage 8 (y [ī], ow [ō], ew, oy)	22
Test passage 9 (au, ī, ou [ŭ], a [ŏ])	24
Test passage 10 (ough, ph, o [ō], are [air])	26
Test passage 11 (y [ĭ], ch [k], ie/ei)	28
Test passage 12 (silent letters)	29
Test passage 13 (soft c and soft g)	31
Test passage 14 (tion, ary, able)	32
Test passage 15 (ful, ance/ant, double consonant/short vowel)	34
Test passage 16 (sion, ous, ious, cious)	36
Test passage 17 (our, ly, fully)	37
Test passage 18 (le ent/ence)	39
Revision Dictations	40
Word Family Lists	44
Alphabetical Index	103

Remedial Spelling

Teenagers and adults with spelling difficulties will usually present an unpredictable pattern of spelling development. Experience has taught them something, but experience varies with individuals, so that problems will be random. It is essential therefore, that the teaching of spelling beyond the primary school stage, should be diagnostic. It should also be flexible to suit the needs of the student, not the teacher.

Years of spelling difficulty have often inhibited a student's writing skills and it is possible that dictation passages, both Test and Reinforcement, will be too long for individual students, particularly in the early stages. In each case, use as much of a passage as a student can comfortably manage — and save the rest for revision. If problems are that great, the teacher will constantly need to return to short vowel sounds and early digraphs.

All teaching should be multi-sensory. If these students had a good visual memory, they would certainly not have reached secondary education, or adulthood, with a spelling problem. It is essential therefore, that ears, mouth and hand should support the eyes in the acquisition of spelling. 'Listen to it' — 'Feel it in your mouth' — 'Write it' — will join 'Look at it' — as instructions.

Copying will play no part in the teaching. These students do not learn from copying. I have seen too many teenagers, men and women in the Adult Literacy Scheme, pull out a piece of paper and copy their address, to believe that copying is a positive learning activity for those with literacy problems. They have copied that address hundreds of times, but still cannot throw the piece of paper away.

Dictation requires the student to listen, to process sounds and to record those sounds in symbols. What he can record is the extent of his knowledge. Our aim is to push his spelling skills forward until he can automatically write everything he desires to write.

Spelling skills are extended through teaching in a structured way. Many students believe that there is no pattern to English spelling. There is — and about 85% of words we use conform to a pattern. It is often a great relief for students to know this and to understand that together, you are going to work through the word families that make up the English phonic structure.

Within the structure, they may have random knowledge. Use that knowledge and integrate it. Build the unfamiliar onto the familiar. In this way, memory will be aided and spelling skills will grow.

Test Passages

(a) Dictate Test Passage 1 in short meaningful phrases. Do not read the whole passage to students first, nor allow them to read it.

(b) If possible, the teacher should be able to watch the students writing, in order to note hesitations, alterations, etc.

(c) Students should write in pencil, or erasable pen.

(d) If Test Passage 1 is completed with no mistakes, no hesitations and no alterations, then Test Passage 2 should be presented and so on.

(e) If Test Passage 1 is completed with errors, look at the errors and plan the remediation programme accordingly.

Possible errors

   (i) Short vowel confusion.

   (ii) Consonant blend problems, either omissions, or wrong sequencing.

   (iii) b/d confusion, or capitals used.

   (iv) Problem with 'y' at the beginning of 'yet'.

(f) Record errors made by individual students.

Remediation

(a) If all short vowels are causing problems, then *one* should be taught each week. It is counter-productive to aim to teach more than one word family a week — the muddles of the preceding years will remain.

(b) It is possible that 'a', 'o', and 'i' will be automatically known, leaving 'e' and 'u' to be dealt with. Again, only one of these should be taught a week. 'U' is often the last short vowel to be conquered.

(c) Consonant blends should be taught as *part* of the remediation programme. The student should be trained to feel the sounds in his mouth and then let his mouth tell his hand what to do. It may take several months before this becomes an automatic procedure.

(d) The consonant 'y' is often the last consonant sound to be acquired. Time may need to be spent on *listening* to this as an initial sound and *relating* the sound to the symbol in common words like 'yes', 'yellow', 'yet', 'you', 'yours', 'yesterday'. Students should not write these words; only recognise and write the initial letter.

(e) A b/d problem will not be cured easily and should be tackled as part of the main remediation programme, once a few guidelines have been given.
Perhaps the easiest is 'bed'.
Draw a bed —

$$b\ e\ d$$

If you want to get out you do not kick your toe.

$$d\ e\ b$$

If you want to get out you kick your toe whichever way you go!

Help students to *listen* to the b/d sounds and relate to the symbols. Encourage them to draw their own beds when confused.

Teaching Method

(a) Turn to relevant word family.
(b) Discuss with students the size of the family. With short vowel sounds, families are long, so that once the sound/symbol relationship has been mastered, a number of words are under control. Always draw attention to the common element in the family, do not assume that students will recognise this for themselves. If necessary use a red pen to isolate the common factor
(c) In some families there are only a few common words and it

is often a relief to know that once these are conquered, few others remain.
(e.g. — these, complete, extreme, supreme, theme, scene; — any, many).

(d) Select approximately ten words from a word family list, relevant to the age and interests of students, but also including the harder words in the family dictation passage.
(e.g. 'a' family — Grandad - Gran/dad, sprang, black).

(e) When the selection has been made, dictate the words to the students. They should write in pencil, or erasable pen, onto rough paper. The teacher should, if possible, watch as students write and anticipate failure, saying 'Listen,' or 'Feel it in your mouth,' if the hand appears to be making the wrong movement.

(f) Take the rough paper and dictate the words again into a 'Word Family Book'. This should be a small (4" x 6" — 10cm x 16cm) note-book. In the early stages pencil, or erasable pen should be used.
Only *one* word family to a page. Other words can then be added to the family if necessary.

(g) For homework, these words should be *read aloud* daily — not sounded out, or copied out, just read.

(h) Next lesson, take a separate exercise book and give the dictation relevant to that word family. The teacher should give as much help as possible through the voice.

(i) Only as many sentences as the student can comfortably write, should be given. Other sentences in the passage can be used for revision, so space should be left in the note-book if the passage is not completed.

(j) Notes will be found under dictation passages, related to basic words (often non-phonic) and spelling rules. Not all students will present the same problems and teachers will therefore have to tackle them as they arise, until individual difficulties have been diagnosed. Then, teaching should precede dictation and therefore failure could be prevented.

(k) Teach next word family.
If all necessary word families have been taught, move on to

reinforcement passages, using as much as the student can comfortably write.

(l) When all reinforcement passages have been successfully covered, move on to the next Test Passage.
Diagnose, teach and reinforce in the same manner, until all Test Passages have been completed.

(m) Move on to Section B.

Revision

If problems remain with individual word families, particularly short vowels, spend time in revision before moving on. Confusion may have lasted for years and needs to be resolved.

When revising, remind student of word family and add extra words to the list, dictating as before.

Students should read sentences already written in a previous lesson and teacher should then continue dictation.

Should it be necessary, further sentences can be made up by student/teacher, relevant to the word family.

Basic Words

These words, such as 'they', 'said', 'one', do not conform to a phonic pattern and have probably been wrongly spelt for years, so that the hand needs to be retrained.

Discuss with students the part of the word that is always wrong (thay/they, sed/said) and suggest that they should always verbalise about the problem before writing one of these words, so that mouths are telling hands what to do.

If necessary, use a finger tracing method to retrain hand movements, verbalising as the action takes place.

Words which are essential to the student, (name, address, written form of numbers, days of the week, months of the year, technical words) can be tackled in this way *before* they are reached phonically, or if they are odd words and will never slot into a word family.

Spelling Rules

Do not overload students with rules that they will neither remember, nor satisfactorily apply under pressure. A few rules help.

(a) Double consonants usually follow short vowels (dinner/dining, hopping/hoping, latter/later).

(b) 'It's' is short for 'it is'. If this is taught, then the possessive 'its', can always be considered as 'the other one', without too much difficulty.

(c) Generally, it is better to teach the apostrophe indicating missing letters, before placing too much stress on its use in the possessive position (that's, don't, I've, haven't etc.).

(d) Usually, a soft 'c', or 'g', is followed by an 'e', 'i' or, 'y'.

Test Passage 1 — (short vowels)

The man went to rob the bank. He had a gun and a bag. At the bank, six bells began to ring. He did not stop, but ran from the bank up the hill. He left the gun and his black bag next to the lift. A clock struck ten and he felt a bump, as a strong dog sprang at him. Yet, he did not stop.

If necessary teach:

a (page 44)

   Grandad had his black cap on and a bag of sand in his hand. The bad, fat cat sprang at him.

o (page 45)

   Tom had a job in the hot dog van. He got cramp in his hand and lost a lot of the hot dogs from the top of a box. His boss was cross.

i (page 46)

   They had crisps, soft drinks and salad for a picnic. It was hot and still and they sat on the hill. Tim had a swift sting on his fist, as he had a long drink from a tin.

e (page 48)

   Helen went to the dentist. She rang the bell and then sat next to seven men. She felt a bit sick, left her red bag and went to get help at the desk.

u (page 49)

   Mum has mumps, so she must not go to the club on the bus. It's not much fun just to dust and scrub. She is upset at her bad luck. It's unjust to get the lumps and bumps of mumps as an adult.
   Note: Remind — it's (it is).

Reinforcement 1

(a) Nick felt upset. He did not expect the gas, the electric and the tax bills to be prompt. He was ill and had no extra funds in the bank. He struck the bed with his fist in disgust. He must sell his trumpet to get the cash.
   Note: ck, sh, and the end of 'extra'.

(b) Mrs. Smith saw the taxi crash into the fish shop. With a rush, she shot back, just as a dish of shrimps fell from a

shelf. There was a crash and a splash on the cash desk. She had a gash on her shin from the dish.
Note: sh, th, and ending of 'tax<u>i</u>'. Discuss 'there'.

(c) The kidnap gang dumped Miss Smith into the vivid red van. She felt sick at the unexpected bump and the smell of the pig filth on the planks of the van. She began to suspect, with disgust, that they sprang the trap for the drugs in her bag. Then jet-lag swept across her and she slept.
Note: they, for and 'ed' ending.

(d) The French band had lunch at the fish and chip shop. They sang pop songs, as they munched fish and chicken with chips. Children stopped to chat and sat next to them on a bench. When they had finished lunch, the Frenchmen gave the children a bag of chestnuts to crunch. Then they shot off in a red and black van.
Note:
   (i) double consonant/short vowel (stopped).
   (ii) 'ed' (munched, finished).
   (iii) Point out ending in 'child<u>re</u>n'.

Test Passage 2 (ee, oo, or, ar)

At the weekend, the Queen went across the park in a green jeep. She had on a scarlet scarf and cardigan. A zoo is at the north end of the park and the Queen had a good look at it. Visitors to the zoo stood on steep banks to see her. A horse took corn from her hand, then, at noon, a storm began. The Queen was swept off in a car, at speed, so that the visitors could not meet her.

If necessary teach:

ee (page 51)
   Free gifts of beef were seen on the TV screen. Mr. Street went at speed in his van up the steep hill to the shop. He had been asleep, when Mrs. Street dragged him to his feet and sat him at the wheel. As the van stopped at the shop, he could see he had missed the free beef for the week.
Note:
   (i) Double consonant/short vowel — dragged, stopped, missed.

10

(ii) Basic words — were, could.

(iii) Mr., Mrs., TV.

oo (page 52)

Bill took the food to his bedroom. He tripped on a broom and dropped his spoon. As he stooped to pick it up, his foot slipped. The food crashed. He took a good look at the mess and then sat on his bed in his gloomy room to see TV.
Note:

(i) Double consonant/short vowel — dropped, tripped.

(ii) ck, sh.

(iii) y ending ($\bar{e}$) — gloomy.

ar (page 53)

Charles banged his arm in the car-park. It was dark and he did not see the sharp wooden bar across the wet tar. His dog started barking and darted across the tar to the market. Charles wished he had parked in a No Parking spot.
Note:

(i) ed.

(ii) mark<u>et</u>, woode<u>n</u>.

or (page 54)

The visitor from the north was on platform one, but she forgot that the doctor was to meet her on platform three. She rushed off to the car-park and had a good look for his car. With alarm, she saw it was not there and she began to feel angry. Then a horn tooted and the doctor's car shot across the yard.
Note:

(i) 'one' — discuss spelling.

(ii) y ending ($\bar{e}$) — angry.

(iii) Basic word — there.

(iv) doctor's — possessive 's'.

Reinforcement 2

(a) Forty cooks had been cooking food for the Queen. When she left in her large car, they fell asleep on the green carpet in the bar. They didn't need beds in smart bedrooms. It had been a long hard morning, but they had seen the Queen.
Note: didn't (did not).

(b) The speed limit on the steep hill was marked as forty, for there were many sharp bends. The dark man at the wheel of the sports car forgot, and rushed on to the car-park along the street. The car hit a tree and landed in a garden.
Note:
 (i) Basic words — there, were, many.
 (ii) gard<u>e</u>n.
(c) On the TV screen at the week end, a doctor on a horse, set a record. He rushed into a yard and shot darts at a scarlet target. He soon cut the target into forty parts, and handed them to the visitors in the yard. The scarlet target was a large jam tart.
(d) The alarm rang and the men sorting tools, stopped. They ran into the dark yard, but did not see the sparks on the roof of the barn. A storm had torn up trees and split a steel platform. This struck the barn roof and hundreds of sparks shot up.

Test Passage 3 — (long vowel/silent e)
The plane took off and the man went to shave. His wife sat alone and began to wipe the make-up from her nose. She took her huge, blue bag and looked inside. She started to fume and shake when she saw that her white make-up case was not there, but at home. She closed the blue bag and was quite rude to her husband when he came back to sit beside her.
Note: Watch basic words 'off' and 'there'.

If necessary teach:
a-e (page 58)
 The cave was not safe, but the brave doctor went in to save Mr. and Mrs. Frame. She took a spade and her case. A gale made it hard and as it was late, it was dark. The doctor did not give her name, nor did she blame the Frames for going into the cave.
i-e (page 60)
 The fireman went on his bike to a fire at the wine-bar. It was quite a ride and took a long time. He picked up a pile of white ice and went inside to the blaze. Then the bar-man gave him nine plum pies, nineteen knives, ninety plates and

five prize wines to take home to his wife. They were nice, but black from the fire.

Note:
   (i) ck — short vowel (black, pick)
   (ii) 'ed' ending (picked).

o-e (page 62)
The cook at the hotel broke his nose. He chose to go home alone and not to the doctor. He left home-made scones on the stove and wrote a note for the hotel visitors. They phoned him at home and spoke to his wife. The hotel closed for lunch, so they went to a motel.

u-e (page 63)
The blue tube of glue was a clue to the crime, but the policemen did not see it. They took a black pipe and a huge white cube with them and went to queue for the phone. They began to argue with the men in the queue, who were, in fact, quite rude.

Note:
   (i) Link 'police' with 'ice' family.
   (ii) Look at 'queue' as 'ue'-'ue'.
   (iii) Discuss 'who' before dictation.

Reinforcement 3

(a) It was not safe to skate at the ice-rink as the hot sun had made the ice melt. The gates were closed and many in the queue did not like it. They began to blame the hopeless rules and not the hot sunshine. They stood in the shade beside the gate and would not drive the long miles home. They still hoped to skate on the ice.

Note:
   (i) 'Many' and 'would'.
   (ii) Remind *one* consonant/long vowel (hoped).

(b) Tom Jones woke up at nine and had cornflakes and coffee. The milkman was late and Tom used all of the milk. He wrote a note for the milkman and said his wife would like five cartons of milk. He left the note, with some change, at the back gate. He closed the gate and drove off along the lane.

Note: Discuss 'coffee', 'said' and 'some' before dictation.

(c) The bride arrived late and the bridegroom stood quite alone looking brave. He smiled as she came in, but his hands began to shake. He spoke to her in a soft tone and seemed to make a joke. Her face changed and she smiled. She gave him a white rose and a safety pin.

(d) The lame horse limped up the hill. It was a steep slope and he began to slide back. Nineteen other horses in the race chased by in a long line. They had five miles to go and then one of them would win the prize. The lame horse had no hope, so went home and did not continue the race.
Note: Discuss 'other' and 'one' before dictation.

Test Passage 4 (ai, oa, ir, ou)

Thirty girls stood and waited for the train in the rain. There was no waiting-room, so they were outside on the platform. Some began to moan and others to shout as the rain soaked their coats and made them dirty. They were going to catch the boat and were afraid they would miss it. The train came just as hail fell from a huge, black cloud. They stopped moaning and shouting and rushed to get on the train first.
Note:
- (i) Watch also 'tch' (catch) and double consonant/short vowel (stopped).
- (ii) If necessary teach 'their' (ignore 'there' until a later date).

If necessary teach:

ai (page 64)

The paint on the main drain-pipe was wet and as the snail crept along, it got stuck. It seemed to be in pain as it lifted its tail. But how can a snail complain about the pain of being stuck on wet paint?

Note: Discuss 'its' before dictation and link with 'their'.

oa (page 66)

The boat began to float along the coast. It was loaded with coal from the coal-mine. The men from the pit went to a cloakroom to get rid of the coal dust with soap. Then they went back along the road for hot toast and coffee, to get rid of the coal dust in their throats.
Note: Remind — 'their' and 'coffee'.

ir (page 67)
The girl went to the circus on her third birthday. She had on a nice blue skirt and coat. She was thirsty and had a tin of fizzy drink. It squirted onto her blue skirt and onto the shirt of the man next to her. He looked cross and she was sad, as her blue skirt was not quite as nice.
Note: Remind double consonant/short vowel — 'fizzy'.

ou (page 68)
The mouse crept round the outside of the house without making a sound. The housewife went out of the lounge to hang her blouse on the line. She found the mouse, gave a loud shout and dropped the blouse.
Note:
  (i) Discuss dropping 'e' to add 'ing' in 'making' — before dictation.
  (ii) Remind — double consonant/short vowel — 'dropped'.

Reinforcement 4

(a) The goal went into the net and loud shouts went up around the ground. A back fell onto the pitch with a moan. He held his knee and the coach ran on with the first-aid bag. It looked as if the chap had a bad sprain. He limped off and the game continued. The score was two goals to nil.
Note:
  (i) Remind — 'tch' (pitch, catch).
  (ii) Remind — silent 'k' in knee.
  (iii) Link 'continued' with 'blue', 'glue' etc.
  (iv) Link 'score' with 'or' family.

(b) The girl had a sore throat, which was very painful. She went to the doctor and moaned when he looked in her mouth. He explained that the pain was due to strain. She must rest her throat and gargle daily.
Note:
  (i) Link 'sore' with 'score' and 'due' with 'blue'.
  (ii) One 'l' when 'full' is at the end of a word (painful).
  (iii) Discuss 'le' ending of 'gargle'. If the 'e' were next to the 'g' it would be soft.

(c) When they got off the boat, they drove south along the mountain road, until they came to a roundabout. They took

the road to the left and hoped it went back to the coast. For a long time it wound round and round and they felt hungry, thirsty and lost. Then, the wife gave a shout as she found they had come round in a circle.
Note:
  (i) Remind — 'off'
  (ii) Remind — one consonant/long vowel (hoped).
  (iii) Discuss ending of 'circle'. If the 'e' were next to the 'c' it would be soft.

(d) The man waved as the boat set sail to cross the Atlantic. He put his arm round his wife's waist and they smiled at those standing ashore. He had made the crossing before, but it was her first trip. They rounded the coast and sailed against the tide into the wind.
Note:
  (i) Link 'ashore' and 'before' with 'sore' and 'score'.
  (ii) Check spelling of Atlantic and remind of capital letter.

Test Passage 5 (ea [ē], ay, ur, aw)

The holiday began on Saturday and the family went away by train to the sea. They took a picnic meal of meat sandwiches, with peanuts and crisps. For a treat, they had peaches, but without cream. The train crawled along and it was awful. They yawned in turn and were glad to play a game with playing cards on the seat. Then Mum saw the church by the stream. They quickly packed up the cards and were pleased to leave the train.

Note: Also pay attention to spelling of 'family' and 'sandwiches'.

If necessary teach:
ea [ē] (page 69)
  It was hot and they sat on the beach each day. They ran in and out of the sea and didn't feel the heat. Mum and Dad found a seat in the shade so that they could read. At tea-time, they went back to the flat for a meal of meat, peas and beans. Then they had ice-cream with peaches, or treacle tart.
  Note
    (i) Discuss 'didn't' (did not).
    (ii) Discuss 'le' ending of 'treacle'. Link with 'circle'.

ay (page 71)
> On Tuesday, Dad had to go away for the day to collect his pay. When he came back he gave them a plastic bag with books, crayons, and clay in it. But it was time for bed, so they couldn't play until Wednesday.
> *Note:*
> (i) Discuss T<u>ue</u>sday and link with blue.
> (ii) Discuss Wednesday — Wed-nes-day.
> (iii) Discuss couldn't (could not).

ur (page 72)
> The nurse put on her fur coat. She took her purse and went out to buy a turkey. It was Thursday today and her visitors were coming on Saturday. They could have peas and turnips with the meat.
> *Note:* Discuss the 'u' in 'buy'

aw (page 73)
> As the man sat on the lawn, he saw the straw begin to burn. There was an awful smell. He got up, just as the baby began to crawl across to the burning straw. The dog put out its paw to draw her away.
> *Note:* Remind — 'its'.

Reinforcement 5

(a) His jeans and jacket were very wet when he got home. He felt awful and his mother wasn't pleased. He took his jeans off and put them on the stove. As he drank a cup of tea, he saw them steaming away. Then his mother burst in to see what was burning. She was even less pleased.
Note:
  (i) Discuss 'jack<u>e</u>t'.
  (ii) Discuss wasn't (was not).
  (iii) Remind to listen for 'off'.

(b) A burglar crawled into a house in the suburbs. The family were away for the day. When they returned, they saw, with surprise, that the curtains had been disturbed. Then, as they went in, they saw the awful mess that the burglar had left. Father rang 999 and said it was urgent. Their house had had an unlawful visitor.

Note:
- (i) Look at the end of 'curtain', 'burglar', and 'urgent'.
- (ii) Remind — 'their'.
- (iii) Remind — only one 'l' when 'ful' is at the end of a word (awful and unlawful).

(c) When the men went to collect their pay, they each had to fill in a form with their first name and surname, before the girl would pay them. They saw no sense in this awful delay. But they liked the girl with her big, blue eyes and black curls. They were pleased to speak to her and tease her.
Note:
- (i) Remind — double consonant/short vowel (collect).
- (ii) Discuss spelling of 'eyes'.

(d) The fishermen went to Norway on a prawn fishing holiday. They began to play leap-frog on the deck and one of them went sprawling. He had to have urgent treatment for a broken arm. A surgeon told him that he was lucky it wasn't his jaw, or his neck with such a stupid display on a wet surface.
Note:
- (i) Discuss need for 'e' in 'surgeon' and link with 'urgent'. ('e', 'i' and 'y', usually, make 'g' soft).
- (ii) Discuss 'surface' (sur/face).

Test Passage 6 (oi, er, all, al, ea [ĕ])

A number of drivers do not remember to halt at the roundabout by the public toilets. Instead, they swerve to avoid cars already there and almost hit the kerb as they speed ahead. It's bad in summer, but in winter it's dreadful, when the weather is frosty and foggy. Local drivers avoid the point altogether, as they understand the danger.
Note: Remind — it's (it is).

If necessary teach:
oi (page 73)
The noisy voice on the coach went on and on. It spoilt the day for everyone. No one could avoid the endless chatter and they went home disappointed. If they had a choice, the noisy spoil-sport would not come on the next trip.
Note: Remind — double consonant/short vowel (chatter).

er (page 74)
> Her sister did not remember to bring the letter when she came to supper yesterday. It did not matter as Mrs. Silver had ordered a paper. This was delivered, so that she could read for herself the advert about the murder on the Underground.
>
> *Note:* Do *not* remind, prior to dictation, about double consonant/short vowel, but watch — 'letter', 'supper' and 'matter'. Prompt, if necessary, by saying — "Think — what do you need?"

all/al (page 76)
> *Before dictation starts, remind that only one 'l' is needed, if another consonant is following and if 'al' comes as a final syllable.*
>
> The stalls were almost perfect when the royal visitors entered the hall. The tall Prince, with his small Princess began walking and talking to all of the helpers. As always, it was a proud moment and a number said that it was, altogether, a most thrilling day.
>
> *Note:*
> (i) Remind — one consonant/long vowel (moment)
> — two consonants/short vowel (thrilling).
> (ii) Remind — 'said'.

ea |ĕ| (page 77)
> In the car headlamps, the headmistress could see that the man in the leather jacket had a weapon. She held her breath and her hands began to sweat. She waited for him to threaten her.
>
> *Note:* Discuss end of 'jacket', 'threaten' and 'weapon'.

Reinforcement 6
(a) The poison in the ointment looked like oil and already healthy dogs were being infected. All of the foil boxes were recalled, but some Germans who had ordered the ointment, did not understand the English letter. A number went ahead and spread the dreadful poison, with its germs, onto their pets.

Note:
   (i) Remind — 'its' and 'their'.

(ii) Remind — only one 'l' when 'ful' is at the end of a word (dreadful).

(b) The barber was angry about the noise his partners made. It gave him such a headache. He was ready to walk out, but he was not a wealthy person and his wife had not been healthy since September. So, he had no choice. He had to stay. Perhaps they would be different if he whispered a threat about walking out?
Note:
   (i) Discuss 'ache' (headache). Link also with stom<u>ach</u> <u>ache</u>.
   (ii) Point out the *three* hazards in 'different' — 'ff', 'er' and 'ent'.
   (iii) Draw attention to 'wh' in whispered.

(c) It is only a small supermarket, so there is little choice of joints of meat. They have the usual things like bread, sandwich spread, salt and pepper, and salad oil. But they have very little that is interesting on offer. In fact, when the shop opened in the summer, it was quite a disappointment.
Note: Remind — one consonant/long vowel (supermarket) — two consonants/short vowel (pepper, summer, offer).

(d) The passenger service on the Underground is meant to be good. The adverts offer steady, noiseless trains, with perfect drivers in summer and winter. To avoid disappointment, it is better to remember that the Underground serves thousands as they travel from shops and streets, trains and buses, to their homes all over the capital.
Note:
   (i) Point out 'ice' ending to service. Link with 'police'.
   (ii) Point out 'e' in 'nois<u>e</u>less'.

Test Passage 7 (ow, igh, a [ar], o [ŭ])

At midnight on Monday, the clown gave a sigh and went to have a bath. His brother went for a shower, but his father ran out into the dark night to look for their mother. She had rushed down the nasty path, away from the bright lights and might have run after the crowds, back into the town. The row between the men had made her frown and the fight had frightened her. She did not want to discover which son had won.

If necessary teach:

ow (page 78)
> The brown owl sat on the church tower in the town. It seemed drowsy and did not lift its head as the prowler in the black gown threatened it with a trowel. The prowler then took a flowered towel and put it over the drowsy owl.
> *Note:* Discuss 'en' in threat<u>en</u>ed.

igh (page 79)
> The flight home was delightful. There was no thunder and lightning to frighten us, and we did not have to sit tight in our seats whilst the plane bumped around in the dark night, fighting the wind and the rain.
> *Note:* Watch for the ending of 'delightful'. Warn — "Think" — if necessary.

a | ar | (page 80)
> The headmaster had a first class breakfast in the staffroom and then went to unfasten the gate by the path to the underpass. One of the fathers was coming to cut the grass, but it was rather wet and he might have to ask him to do it after half-term.

o | ŭ | (page 81)
> Mother went to London on Monday to visit her brother. She left dinner in the oven for her son, but he arrived home late and when he opened the front door, all he could smell was burnt onions. A sponge cake she had left was like burnt toast.
> *Note:* Watch for the 'nn' in dinner. If necessary — warn.

Reinforcement 7

(a) Another heavy shower made the fast cars slow down. The old man gave a sigh. His eyesight was not good in the twilight and the fast cars frightened him. At last, he unfastened his gate and walked along the grass path to his front door. It was wonderful not to worry any more about the nasty, fast traffic on this frightful night.
Note: Watch for the 'ff' in traffic.

(b) The dancer had travelled on a first class flight from France to dance in London tonight. Now, her tights felt too tight over her thighs, and she felt too drowsy to go onto the stage

and dance. The brass began to play and someone gave her a shove. Perhaps it would be all right on the night!
Note: Discuss one 'l' on travel, but double 'l' in travelled.

(c) The lights in the front room went out and there seemed to be no power coming from the power point. Mother took a lamp into the other room to discover whether another power point was all right. However, after fighting her way across the dark room and discovering the power point, the lights suddenly came on.
Note:
  (i) Discuss the hazards of 'whether' — 'wh' and 'e'.
  (ii) Notice double 'dd' in 'sudden' and also the 'e'.

(d) The monkey danced along the branch away from the bright lights. He howled and cowered in a corner as a dozen nasty children frightened him. A passing master from their school scowled at them and they rushed off to worry another animal. The master gave a sigh and vowed he would never bring his class to London Zoo again.

Test Passage 8 (y [ī], ow [ō], ew, oy)

The shy boy threw his yellow bicycle down by the narrow step. He grabbed a dry newspaper and pushed open the gate with his elbow. He flew up the garden path trying not to see the widow's face at the window. He was annoyed. He did not want her to spy on him. He was employed to deliver newspapers and did not want to go inside the house and talk. She gave him chewing-gum, but he didn't enjoy it.

If necessary teach:

y [ī] (page 82)
  The shy spy got onto his bicycle and rode off to meet his contact by the pylons. He forgot that he still had on his pink nylon pyjamas and wondered why the people walking by gasped at the sight of him.
  Note: Discuss 'people' and the position of the 'e'.

ow [ō] (page 83)
  They began to grow tired of throwing snowballs and started to make a snowman. But the wind began to blow and the soft snow slowly became hard. Lights glowed in the windows

and so they followed the grown-ups home, hoping the snow would be soft again tomorrow.
Note:
(i) Link 'tire' with 'fire' and add 'd'.
(ii) Discuss dropping 'e' from 'hope' and adding 'ing' for hoping. Remind — one 'p' — long vowel.

ew (page 84)
The stewards in the plane crew were all chewing chewing-gum. They knew it was not allowed. A new stewardess spoke to them and they threw it down onto some newspaper as the plane flew down to land.

oy (page 84)
The boys went for a joy-ride in their employer's car and destroyed it in a crash. The employer was so annoyed that he rang their parents and informed them that he no longer wished to employ the boys. The parents were annoyed to think that the boys were now unemployed.
Note:
(i) Watch 'their' and warn — "Think" if necessary.
(ii) Discuss 'parents' — draw attention to 'are'.
(iii) Discuss apostrophe 's (employer's).

Reinforcement 8
(a) The new owner of the rowing boat borrowed a nylon tow rope and a screwdriver. He fixed a screw into a narrow bar on his car and slowly towed the boat away from the showroom. He gave a royal wave and shouted goodbye to the fellow standing by the window.

(b) The crew of the yellow van continue to deny that they have stolen the royal jewels. They admit that they had a blowlamp in the van, but say that they had borrowed this from their employer to mend a boy's tricycle. The owner of the blowlamp states that he did not know they had borrowed it. Newspapers say that a blowlamp and a screwdriver had been used on the royal safe before the jewels were stolen.
Note: Discuss 'stolen' and link with silent 'e' family.

(c) English bowlers slowly bowled out the New Zealand batsmen. The crowd seemed to enjoy the game, but I began to get annoyed at the slow pace they threw the balls. I think

there is more enjoyment in a game with more speed. In fact, I know that I could throw those balls better myself. Perhaps I am being disloyal.
Note: Link 'pace' with 'face'.

(d) Below the pylon, in a hollow, some yellow marrows were growing. No one quite knew how they got into the middle of a meadow. However, the boys used to come out on their cycles to look at them and, before the marrows grew very big, drew thin marks on them. When they were fully grown, the thin marks became the names of the boys and they each enjoyed picking their own marrow.

Test Passage 9 (au, ī, ou [ŭ] a [ŏ])

One Friday in August, a young child swallowed a wasp. He had just climbed onto his bicycle, when the wasp touched his younger sister. He wanted to squash it and a squabble started. He shouted at her and touched the wasp from behind. It flew into his open mouth. The trouble was, he then shut his mouth and swallowed. It was not his fault and was really quite automatic.

au (page 85)

The saucepan on the cooker seemed to be haunted. As the sauce boiled, the saucepan hopped around. The author put a saucer on top, but that was no better. The cause was a fault in the bottom of the saucepan, not the top.
Note:
  (i) Before dictation, link end of 'author', with 'doctor' and 'visitor'.
  (ii) Watch double consonant in 'hopped', 'better' and 'bottom'. Warn "Think" if necessary.

ī (page 86)

The wild tiger sat behind the fence, as the tiny child began to climb it. The tiger was silent and the mother, sitting with the child on the private island, did not seem to mind. A kind man on a bicycle rushed up and grabbed the child. He knew the mother was blind.
Note:
  (i) Before dictation, link end of 'private' with silent 'e' family — (ate).

(ii) Discuss end of 'silent'.

(iii) Watch double consonants in 'sitting' and 'grabbed'.

ou |ŭ| (page 87)

The young couple booked a double room at the country hotel. They wanted a nourishing meal, but the trouble was, the only food was at the bar. The young couple wouldn't touch it.

Note:

(i) Remind — 'wouldn't' (would not).

(ii) Discuss 'only'.

a |ŏ| (page 87)

Mother wanted some washing powder for the washing machine. She was swamped with washing and had no time to wander down to the shops. The quads were squabbling about orange squash, so she sent them.

Note: Discuss 'machine'. It sometimes helps to cheat with speech — măc/hine.

Reinforcement 9

(a) The automatic laundry is next to the library, which is by the lido. If you take your washing and put it into a washing machine, the owner of the laundry will watch it, then iron it. You can spend a couple of hours in the library and the lido, before going back to fetch it.

Note:

(i) Remind — 'tch' (watch, fetch).

(ii) Discuss ending of 'library'.

(iii) Discuss 'iron' — 'r' is the problem.

(b) The pirate on the island was wild. He had had a quarrel with a young man on a hijacked yacht. Then, when he wasn't watching, the young man had pinched his haul of diamonds and sailed off. The hijacker taunted the pirate from the deck, as the yacht left the shore behind.

Note:

(i) 'rr' and 'el' in 'quarrel'.

(ii) 'ch' in 'yacht'.

(c) Last autumn, wandering in the countryside, I saw a lake with a tiny island in the middle of it. The trouble was, that there was a swamp between the path and the lake, so it seemed impossible to get to the island. The wildlife must have enjoyed this. The lake was ideal for wild ducks and swans.

Note:
   (i) Remind of 'n' on 'autumn'.
   (ii) Watch 'dd' in 'middle'.

(d) The young author returned to Australia and wanted to talk about his travels in other countries. He had kept a diary to remind him of his wanderings. What he needed, was an audience. He couldn't seem to find one, because he had no friends ready to listen.

Note: Discuss silent letters in 'friends' and 'listen'.

Test Passage 10 (ough, ph, o [ō], are [air])

Although the postman brought the photo soon after the telephone call, the parents did not dare to tell the police about it. They were both scared, so told nobody. They thought their son had sent the photo. They were both old and did not dare to share their tough secret. It was bad enough reading about their nephew in the *Telegraph* and quite thoughtless of the boys to send the photograph of the caretaker to them.

ough (page 88)

He fought the cough throughout the weekend and then bought some cough medicine. Although he had not bought enough, the roughness in his chest was better. He ought to have bought the medicine before, but thought it would be all right.

Note
   (i) Discuss 'medicine'.
   (ii) Look at all possibilities of 'ough' before giving dictation.
   (iii) Watch — double consonant in 'better'.

ph (page 89)

My nephew Philip looked up my phone number in the telephone book. He is only six but knows the alphabet. He phoned me and told me that he had been to the zoo, and had a ride on an elephant. He would send me a photograph.

o [ō] (page 90)

It was so cold in November that the police took the old postman into a local pub. They bought him hot chocolate and a jacket potato. Nobody told the old man that he was a local postman a long time ago. Now, he only walked through the streets with an empty bag. He had no letters and nowhere to go.

are [air] (page 92)

The careful caretaker was aware that he dare not be careless with the bare wires. He was scared that he might get an electric shock. There was a sudden flare and a bright light glared down on the parents in the square hall. They stared up at him, unaware of the cause of the flare.

Note: Link 'wire' with silent 'e' family.

Reinforcement 10

(a) In November, parents often have photographs taken of their children, as presents for grandparents. This is a thoughtful present and most grandparents are aware of the cost in time and money. Sometimes the children are told by their parents to autograph the back of the photo.

Note: Remind — one 'l' on 'full' at the end of a word (thoughtful).

(b) Although my nephew was scared of the elephant, he brought it into the town square. He spoke through the microphone to the crowd, asking for money for those starving through drought. Then he had a photograph taken and the reporter wrote a paragraph about him in the local paper. Everyone was aware that it was a tough job begging for money throughout the country.

(c) The old man finished reading the biography and carefully shut the book. He had thoroughly enjoyed it. Now he thought about his own life. He was an orphan and then, when he was older, became a school caretaker. He had lots of stories that he could share, but did not dare to write his autobiography.

Note:
  (i) Discuss meanings of biography and autobiography.
  (ii) Discuss ending of 'stories'. (Change 'y' to 'i' and add 'es').

(d) The policeman on his motorbike began to cough. The bike shook and ploughed through a telephone kiosk into a field, and hit a scarecrow. A mare stopped eating grass and stared at him. The policeman was unhurt, but very thoughtful, as he stood up on the rough grass. He took hold of his motorbike and was glad that nobody saw the catastrophe.

Note: Discuss spelling of 'kiosk'.

Test Passage 11 (y [ĭ], ch [k], ie/ei)

At Christmas the choir sang hymns in the school gym. Christopher put his handkerchief over his face and gave a loud shriek. The physics master took Christopher out of the gym to solve the mystery of the shriek. Was it mischief, or had he got a headache, or stomach ache? Christopher said that a piece of gym ceiling had dropped on his head. He didn't receive any sympathy from the physics master.

y [ĭ] (page 82)

> It was a mystery how the cough syrup got onto the pyjamas. Mother was not very sympathetic, as she was rushing off to the gym. She thought the rhythm group had been playing with a syringe and anyway, he didn't have the symptoms of a cough, or cold, so didn't need the syrup.

ch [k] (page 56)

> Christine went to the chemist on the way to school. She had a stomach ache. Things had been chaotic at home since Christmas and baby Christopher had been christened on Sunday. She had a scheme about not going to school and wanted to talk to the chemist.

ie/ei ('i' before 'e' *except* after 'c')

> My niece sat on her handkerchief in the field, waiting to receive a piece of cake. She was always up to mischief and her mother could not believe how good she had been on the picnic.

Reinforcement 11

(a) The thief was relieved to see the crystal ball on the mantelpiece. He was a bad character and left the house in chaos as he crept out. He had no sympathy for the family, even though it was Christmas time.

(b) The chief architect was very conceited. He did not believe that the choir and orchestra had found a loud echo in his

new hall. He though it was the school headmaster making mischief.
Note: Discuss the job of an architect.

(c) The chemist won a technical scholarship to America. He was a good gymnast and also played in an orchestra. He believed he would be able to play the cymbals in a rhythm group, if the chief chemist gave him the time off.

(d) The fierce animal crept round the pyramid in Egypt. It was a mystery how it had got there. The visitors to the pyramid were under siege and could not get out of their coach. At last, men came with guns and shot the fierce animal in the stomach.
Note: Talk about Egypt and the pyramids if these are unfamiliar to the students.

Test Passage 12 (silent letters)

The builder knocked on the door and listened. There was no answer, so he thought something was wrong. He unfastened the door and gave a short whistle. There was still no sign of anyone. He had written to say he was coming and knew that the scientist would be at home today, although he was often out.

wr (page 94)

When the BBC wrote to the wrestler, he wanted to phone them with his answer, because he did not like writing letters. His solicitor told him that would be wrong, so he had to write an answer. The BBC then had a written contract signed by the wrestler.
Note:
  (i) Discuss spelling of soli<u>citor</u>. Link end with 'doctor' and visitor.
  (ii) Discuss the importance of contracts.

u (bu, cu, gu) (page 94)

The builder felt guilty as he put the biscuit into his mouth. His tongue guided it to his teeth and then quickly down his throat. No one on the building site could have guessed that he had been eating.

t (page 94)

The guard listened for the whistle and then unfastened the

castle gate. It was not often that guests came to the castle for dinner.

n (page 94)

In the autumn, the cathedral choir sings hymns by the stone column in the castle grounds. The guides are condemned to listen, even if the singing is bad — and often it is. They can then continue the guided tours for the tourists.

Note:
  (i) Discuss ending of 'cathedral'. Link with other words with 'al' ending on page 76.
  (ii) Discuss spelling of tour/tourists.

kn (page 94)

The man knelt down with the knife to mend the door knob. He knew that a knife was the wrong tool, but did not know where to find anything better.

gn (page 94)

The gnat crept up the gnarled trunk of the tree and the gnome signed to the dog to come and gnaw a bone.

sc (page 95)

The scientist took the scissors and began to cut up the scenery. His wife sprayed scent onto her neck and arms.

Reinforcement 12

(a) The builder gave no written guarantee when he built the house for the scientist. Then, one night when it collapsed, he just looked at the wreckage and said that he was not guilty. It was the scientist's poor design that was wrong, not his building.

Note: Discuss the use of guarantees — with specimens. Also the other tricky parts of the spelling — gua<u>r</u>ant<u>ee</u>. Only one 'r' and *double* ee at the end.

(b) The guide ran round the castle wall and knocked over an important guest who was touring the grounds and looking at the scenery. He knew he was wrong to be running. He blew his whistle and the guards came to help. They knelt beside the guest and undid his collar and tie. They condemned the guide for rushing round the wall.

Note: Discuss ending of 'collar' and remind that 'tie' is in silent 'e' family.

Test Passage 13 (soft c and soft g)

George and Georgina were very excited. A message had been received from the manager of the circus, inviting them to accept seats that night. They phoned his office to say that they had decided to accept. The circus was a huge success and received lots of good notices in the papers. But sadly, as they went home, they had an accident and damaged their car. It was only fit for salvage.

Soft c (page 96)

The car began to accelerate round the orange ring. The crowd looked on excitedly, but the driver received some criticism. He failed to notice the circumstances of the other drivers and this could have caused an accident. His accent was on speed.

Note
  (i) Point out — 'c' is usually soft when followed by — 'e', 'i' or 'y'.
  (ii) Look especially at the functions of both 'c's in 'accent' and 'accident' — hard and soft.

Soft g (page 96)

The giant panda went on a gigantic rampage and the damage caused can be left to your imagination. Vegetables were trampled all over the gym floor and the gipsy wished he had never agreed to bring it to the show. He had no knowledge that it would be so unmanageable.

Note: Point out — 'g' is usually soft when followed by 'e', 'i' or 'y'.

Reinforcement 13

(a) Postage has gone up yet again and long queues have formed at the post office. Staff have used a lot of energy trying to make the queues shorter, without success. A message has now been sent to the manager, asking him to imagine what it is like, working under these circumstances.
Note: Remind of spelling of 'queue'. Link with silent 'e' family.

(b) The police sergeant received the medicine and decided to take it to the scene of the accident in the gymnasium. A scientist, who was also an excellent gymnast, had gone to the gym to practise with the rest of the team. During the practice, he had fallen from the trampoline and damaged his spine. Other members of the team were very concerned about the tragedy.

Note:
  (i) Discuss 'to practise' (verb) and 'the practice' (noun). Think about 'practising' — it is often easier to remember the 's' in the verb from this point — and then work backwards!
  (ii) Look especially at the need for the 'e' in sergeant and discuss the 'er' with an unusual sound.

Test Passage 14 (tion, ary, able)

Accommodation near the station was not good, so it was necessary for the young couple to accept invitations to stay separately. They were miserable about the separation, even though it was temporary. They had many conversations about the situation and decided to wait until February to see if accommodation became available over the library. It seemed reasonable to wait, as it was now January, so the prospect was not too disagreeable.

tion (page 97)
  Punctuation was discussed in preparation for the examinations. The master made corrections, held conversations about the repetition of mistakes and then took action over the situation. He insisted that a good education was a preparation for life and that there could be no separation between English written work for school examinations and what was needed for an adult working life.
  Note:
  (i) Discuss 'ar' in 'prep<u>ar</u>ation' and 'sep<u>ar</u>ation'.
  (ii) Remind of double 'rr' in 'correction'.

ary (page 99)
  Some workers in the library were voluntary and some were temporary. It had been like this since February, when it had become necessary for the ordinary workers to have supplementary help. In return for their help, the volunteers did not have to use the ordinary car-park, but were allowed to leave their stationary cars in the space outside the library.

Notes:
   (i) Draw attention to 'r' in 'library' and 'February'.
   (ii) Draw attention to 'or' in 'temporary' and one 'c', double 'ss' in 'necessary'.
   (iii) Discuss meaning of supplementary.
   (iv) Discuss meaning of 'stationary' — as applied to anything that is not moving.

able (page 99)
   The available vegetables were miserable. They were comparable to damaged weeds. But however disagreeable they looked, it was only reasonable to buy them and leave it to the knowledgeable cook to make them look more attractive.
   Note:
   (i) Draw attention to 'e' in 'veget̲ables' and to 'ar' in 'compar̲able'.
   (ii) Point out 'e' in 'knowledge̲able' — to keep 'g' soft.

Reinforcement 14
(a) The conversation in the library about examinations, received an extraordinary interruption. An action committee took up a stationary position outside the window. It was only a temporary stop, but it diverted attention and made conditions in the library most disagreeable.
   Note:
   (i) Draw attention to middle of 'extra/ordinary'.
   (ii) Look at three sets of double letters in committee.
   (iii) Discuss meaning of 'temporary' — including 'temporary accommodation'.

(b) It was necessary for alterations to take place before the temporary accommodation was in a reasonable condition for use. There were a few interruptions to the work, but with supplementary help, the situation improved and only a fraction of time was lost.

(c) In January and February very few fresh vegetables are available. This is because of weather conditions. But, with few exceptions, ordinary people are able to buy reasonable amounts of frozen vegetables, so there are very few objections to this temporary situation.

Test Passage 15 (ful, ance/ant, double consonant/short vowel)

The brilliant and beautiful star slipped out of the elegant dining-room and disappeared into the foggy night. Everyone agreed that her performance in the extravagant show had been delightful, but she was annoyed and embarrassed at the painful and bitter reception she had had at the dinner, due to gossip about her personal life. She was hoping for a wonderful and successful celebration. She had even hoped that she would be announced as the winner of an award.

ful (page 101)

The young man was hopeful of being successful in business. He was truthful, but artful, helpful and skilful. He was a delightful and wonderful character and was expected to fulfil his ambitions. He also had a beautiful wife. It would be wasteful of his ability if he did not succeed.

Note:
(i) Discuss 'beautiful' — make sure student *hears* all of the sounds — bee/u/ti/ful.
(ii) Discuss 'business' — say 'bŭs/i/ness' to remind of slightly difficult spelling.
(iii) Remind — only one 'l', when 'full', 'fill' or 'skill' are followed by another syllable, or are the final syllable.

ance/ant (page 99)

In the circumstances, an alliance between the two acquaintances would be a nuisance. Both were ignorant about the insurance business and needed to apply for vacant positions in other firms, however distant, before making an entrance into this business.

Note:
(i) Talk about beginning of 'acquaintances' ac/quain.
(i) Discuss beginning of 'nuisance'.

Double consonant/short vowel (page 102)

When the traffic came through the tunnel, passengers in the coach wanted to stop for dinner. They saw a hotel with dining accommodation and scribbled a note to the driver. He was annoyed at the thought of leaving the traffic queue. He was beginning to feel very bitter about this difficult collection of passengers and hoped it would never happen again. He would disappear if his boss suggested it.

Note:
(i) Make sure student is *listening* for short and long vowels.
(ii) Talk about 'dis' as a prefix and therefore *not* subject to the rule. 'Diss' only applies if root word begins with 's' (dissatisfaction).

Reinforcement 15

(a) The police sergeant wrote down the accommodation address and said he hoped that it was still vacant, as he thoroughly recommended it. The family collected their luggage and disappeared into the distance. The sergeant was ignorant of their circumstances, but it looked as if they had been having a difficult time.

Note:
(i) Discuss 'ough' in 'thoroughly'.
(ii) Discuss 'family' — one 'm' and 'i' — fam_ily.

(b) The operation was painful, but certainly the surgeon had been very skilful. However, the hospital was some distance from the woman's home and this made it difficult for friends and relations to visit. She was feeling quite miserable when some voluntary helpers came round with the hospital library. They recommended a good narrative from their collection of books. They thought it might be successful in cheering her up.

Note: Discuss need for 'e' in 'surgeon'.

(c) The brilliant scientist collected the apparatus from the laboratory. He knew the others were annoyed about his extravagance in the present difficult circumstances. They thought he was ignorant of the problems, but he was just skilful in keeping his distance from them. He knew that it would be wasteful if the present research was unsuccessful through a lack of suitable apparatus.

Note:
(i) Discuss 'appa_ratus'.
(ii) Discuss 'su_itable' link with 'nu_isance'.

Test Passage 16 (sion, ous, ious, cious)

The famous, professional, first division soccer star, appeared on television for a serious discussion programme. There were no previous meetings about the show and he was obviously anxious and nervous. Viewers were curious to watch the discussion, as it was slightly mysterious as to why he had received an invitation. There was some confusion at the beginning of the programme, but when he settled down, he was marvellous and really quite humorous.

sion (page 98)

There was some discussion about giving permission for the excursion to see the procession. There were fears about an invasion of foreigners into the town. The occasion was meant to be for local people, not outsiders and television cameras. There could be no provision for extra visitors. The council meeting ended in confusion and no decision was reached.

Note: Link 'foreign' and 'foreigner' with 'eight'.

ous (page 97)

The carnivorous animal was not concerned about either coniferous, or deciduous trees. All it wanted was marvellous meat. The villagers were nervous of it. They stopped arguing about trees and started a vigorous campaign to get rid of the mysterious beast. They became quite famous for a time and then the animal disappeared, so they went back to their ridiculous divisions over the planting of new coniferous, or deciduous trees.

Note:
 (i) Discuss meaning of 'carnivorous'.
 (ii) Discuss 'coniferous' and 'deciduous' trees.
 (iii) Point out silent letter in campaign.
 (iv) Point out dropping of 'e' in arguing, before adding ending.

ious/cious (page 97)

Everyone was curious about the mysterious new family who had come to live in the neighbourhood. They seemed industrious and conscientious and no one knew of any previous serious crime they had committed. But, for some

subconscious reason, the villagers were all suspicious of them. It was really quite ridiculous.
Note:
  (i) Link 'neighbour' with 'eight' and 'foreign'.
  (ii) Discuss middle of 'conscientious'.
  (iii) Discuss meanings of 'conscientious' and 'subconscious'.

Reinforcement 16

(a) The mysterious explosion caused confusion amongst the crowd as they stood and waited for the royal procession. People felt nervous and suspicious of those around them. Then the television producer made an announcement over his microphone. The explosion had been caused by an over-industrious electrician in his crew. The nervous crowd cheered at the admission and relaxed in time to enjoy the occasion.
Note: Discuss spelling of 'electrician'. Link 'ci' with 'sh' sound in 'suspicious'.

(b) The porous rock was suffering from atrocious erosion and the situation required action. A famous group of voluntary climbers took the extraordinary decision of mounting an excursion to fence off the area before a serious accident happened. The occasion received a lot of television coverage and produced an admission by the authorities that discussions about the safety of the area had created serious divisions within their committee.
Note: Discuss meanings of 'porous' and 'erosion'.

Test Passage 17 (our, ly, fully)

The behaviour of the fans in the neighbourhood of the harbour was noticeably good. Usually, they disembarked from the ferry particularly noisily. But, as they went to the station to catch trains and coaches, they were especially quiet. Probably their favourite team had successfully reached the final stage of the European Cup. But it might have been that they were encouraged in their good behaviour by the voluntary neighbourhood groups, who stood quietly along the side of the road, definitely trying to discourage trouble.

our (page 98)
>A favourite colour for front doors in the neighbourhood is yellow. The council has tried to encourage a wider choice of colours, but once yellow has been used, it saves a great deal on labour costs if the same colour is repeated. No encouragement to use blues and greens makes any difference at all. Neighbours now think it is a matter of honour to stick to their favourite colour, rather than submit to the council.
>*Note:*
>(i) Point out different American spelling of 'our' words and use an American publication to illustrate this.
>(ii) Remind of need for 'e' in encourag*e*ment.

ly, fully (page 101)
>Finally, the board of directors definitely agreed to gradually introduce voluntary redundancy. Naturally, they were hopeful that nothing would need to happen immediately so that they could quietly discuss the situation truthfully with their managers. But orders were sparse in the family company and really, there was very little opportunity of successfully changing the situation.
>*Note:*
>(i) Point out 'oar' in 'board' and link ending of 'direct*or*' to 'doct*or*', 'visit*or*'.
>(ii) Look at double 'l' in words which end in 'l' before adding suffix 'ly' — gradual/ly, natural/ly, successful/ly, truthful/ly.
>(iii) Discuss need to keep silent 'e' in 'definit*e*ly', 'hop*e*ful', 'immediat*e*ly'.

Reinforcement 17

(a) Obviously the vapour rising from the water in the harbour was partially due to the intensely hot weather. Immediately it became noticeable, the authorities quickly and successfully discouraged visitors to the area whilst they investigated the problem. Their subsequent behaviour probably saved a disaster in the neighbourhood.
Note: Discuss meanings of 'vapour', 'partially' and 'subsequent'.

(b) The family lived quietly in sparsely furnished accommodation. Their neighbours admired their courage and encouraged them to join in local activities, particularly the children. They were naturally musical and excitedly accepted an invitation to join a wind band. Their favourite instruments were brass and immediately things changed. The house became noticeably noisier, as the children gradually gained confidence in their performance on the euphonium and the bass. Fortunately, no one discouraged them and soon all were enjoying the music they were making.

Test Passage 18 (le, ent/ence).

There were arguments in Parliament about experiments on jungle animals. It seemed impossible for members to agree on principles which were really a matter of conscience. There was a persistent campaign from those responsible for the experiments to lobby different prominent ministers. They were certainly not idle, nor unintelligent in the development of their campaign. It would certainly have been irresponsible not to listen, but then to reach an independent decision.

Note: Discuss meanings of 'principles', 'persistent', 'prominent', and 'irresponsible'.

le (page 100)

It is quite probable that the scramble to scribble on walls is the result of innocent boredom. Children with insufficient activity, are likely to doodle whilst they chatter. Unfortunately their idle doodling is not invisible and causes offence to responsible adults.

Note: (i) Discuss 'e' in 'bor<u>e</u>dom' and 'unfortunat<u>e</u>ly'.
 (ii) Listen to 'i' in 'invis<u>i</u>ble' and 'respons<u>i</u>ble'.

ent/ence (page 100)

It was quite a compliment to be invited to attend the magnificent dinner given in honour of the committee who had worked so hard for the development of the town. It had begun as an experiment and few members had any experience in this field. There were some differences of opinion at the commencement of activities, but with persistent, intelligent discussion, the development progressed successfully and efficiently. There was some inconvenience at the start, but this was overcome by patience and good humour.

Note: Discuss meanings of 'persistent' and 'efficient'.

Reinforcement 18

(a) In the announcement, reference was made to the ingredients contained in the sample. There was concern about lack of experiment on some of these ingredients and also the principle of hailing this as a miracle cure. It seemed irresponsible to commence marketing, whilst a sensible period of waiting, might have given time for the development of a more efficient, safer, sample.

(b) Often the difference between obedience and disobedience lies simply in the intelligent, or unintelligent handling of a situation by the responsible adult. Argument can be the accompaniment to a seemingly innocent announcement of future activities. To the child, it seems as if these are purely for the convenience of the adult, without any consideration of his feelings in the circumstances. With a different approach, it is quite probable that the argument would not have developed.

Revision Dictations

*(These dictations should be given when **all** Test Passages have been completed)*

1. My mother won some money on the football pools and decided to buy a new car. Last Tuesday, the whole family went down to the car showrooms to have a look. It was about five o'clock, but the salesmen were still there. Mother thought she would like a small, blue hatchback with an automatic gearbox. We looked around and saw just the car. Father looked at the engine and asked a lot of questions. Then the salesman put some petrol in the tank, we piled in and drove off for a trial. Mum was quite nervous at first, but after a few miles, she settled down and we thoroughly enjoyed the drive. Later, we went back to the garage and she paid by cheque for the car.
    Note: After the dictation, link any mistake with the appropriate word family, or spelling rule and do necessary revision.

2. There was an argument at last night's meeting of the Parent-Teachers Association. One leading member of the committee suggested that extra funds for the school should be raised

through raffles. Others wanted to organise a sponsored walk, so that the children could be involved. Quite heated speeches followed, until a vote was taken. Half of those present voted in favour of the raffle and half in favour of the sponsored walk. The headmaster gave the casting vote for the sponsored walk.

3. My sister and brother-in-law recently arrived home after a three year contract with an oil company in Nigeria. They had some fascinating experiences to share and we spent a considerable amount of time listening. My niece and nephew had attended a Nigerian school and had become quite close friends with local children. Fortunately, their education had been quite traditional, so that they would fit into the local comprehensive school without too much trouble. They all wanted to catch up on news and views about events that had occurred during their period of absence.

4. The college lecturers told a group of students that they had no hope of achieving good grades in their final examinations. They had attended so few lectures that there were large sections of the curriculum that they had not covered. It was irresponsible to accept a local authority grant and financial support from their parents, whilst ignoring the work their course required them to do. It was too late now to reclaim the lost time. They could look forward to years ahead of regret at the wasted opportunities.

5. Members of the local cricket team were extremely disappointed when they heard that their captain would be unable to play for the rest of the season. He had pulled a muscle in his shoulder and the doctor had ordered him to rest. As he was also the opening bat, his absence was bound to have a disastrous effect on the whole team's performance. Certainly, they went on to suffer a depressing number of defeats and were relieved when the autumn and the end of the season came.

6. The residents recently called a meeting to air their views on the condition of the pavements in the High Street. Despite numerous complaints, the local authority had ignored them

and they were now thoroughly annoyed. They pointed out to the local councillors who were present at the meeting, that there had been several accidents caused by the uneven paving stones. They were particularly concerned for the safety of the elderly and the handicapped and wanted a guarantee that something would be done.

7. Members of Parliament regularly meet constituents who wish to enlist their support for bills which are passing through the House of Commons. In a democracy, it is essential that the views of ordinary people, on important national issues, should be taken into account. Many special groups come to discuss unemployment, poverty, pensions and education. Usually, they have an appointment with MPs and are shown through the security checks to the lobby. Frequently there are also guided tours for foreigners, who are sightseeing. They all crowd into the Houses of Parliament and police on duty are kept quite busy controlling queues.

8. The Borough Council engaged two builders to construct an exhibition area in the Leisure Centre. Electricians, technicians, plumbers, carpenters and interior decorators were soon busy transforming the place. An experienced engineer was employed as the organiser of the project and was given a very generous budget. Unfortunately, a series of strikes affected the work schedules and the whole operation was much more expensive than expected. An agency was engaged to sell trade-stand space in the exhibition and advertising in a highly coloured brochure. It was hoped that the revenue produced would off-set the high cost of the venture.

9. Security guards were making a routine check of the airport boundary, when they saw smoke rising from a chemical factory on a nearby industrial estate. They immediately phoned for emergency services, but by the time the fire-engine arrived, the whole building was enveloped in billowing smoke. Explosions could be heard, followed by soaring flames. Police were particularly concerned about danger to approaching aircraft. The decision was taken to ban all

incoming and outgoing flights until the crisis was over. Planes were diverted to other airports causing chaos for the thousands who were awaiting passengers in the terminals.

10. Following the successful launching of the first space rocket to the moon, the President congratulated the brilliant scientists who had made this immense undertaking possible. He had high praise for the astronauts, upon whose courage the success of the venture depended. For them, the cramped conditions of the capsule, the journey into the unknown and the suppressed fears concerning the performance of their craft during its maiden voyage. But, for them also, the triumph of being the first men on the moon. He was honoured to be the President in a period when his fellow countrymen were taking this giant stride towards the conquest of the universe.

Word Family Lists

a

Basic List

am	cramp	hat	sang
an	chat	jam	sat
and	cash	jab	scab
ant	crash	jazz	scraps
as	Dad	land	slam
at	damp	lamp	slap
act	fact	lap	snag
add	fat	man	snap
back	flag	mad	spank
bad	flan	map	spat
bag	flap	mat	sprang
band	flash	nap	stab
bang	flashy	pan	stamp
bank	gag	pants	stand
bat	gap	pat	strap
black	gas	plan	swam
blank	gang	plank	splash
brag	gash	pram	tan
can	grab	ran	tank
cap	grand	rang	tap
camp	Grandad	rag	tax
cat	glad	rat	taxi
clap	had	rap	trap
clamp	ham	ramp	tramp
clang	hand	sad	van
crab	has	sand	wag

Supplementary

abstract	gland	plastic	sprat
clad	Japan	ram	stag
crag	lad	rank	tag
dam	lab	sag	transact
drab	lag	slab	
drag	mass	slang	
franc	pad	span	

o

Basic List

across	from	knot	pop
boss	frock	knob	pot
box	frost	lock	pond
blot	flock	lot	plot
cot	flog	loft	rob
cock	flop	lost	rod
cod	got	loss	rot
cog	gong	long	rock
cost	God	mob	sock
clock	gloss	mop	soft
clog	hot	mock	song
clot	hot-dog	moss	stop
cross	honk	nod	slot
crop	hog	not	spot
dog	hop	odd	strong
doll	hopped	of	swop
dot	hopping	off	shop
drop	job	off-hand	top
fog	jog	on	trot
frog	jot	pod	

Supplementary

bog	plonk	scoff	stock
contact	pomp	Scot	toss
contract	prompt	Scotland	tot
opt	prong	slog	
ox	prop	slop	
plod	romp	snob	

i

Basic List

bib	fit	lipstick	risk
bid	fist	limp	sip
big	fifth	link	sit
bill	filth	lisp	six
bit	fish	list	silk
blink	finish	lick	sing
brick	fix	limit	sink
bring	fizz	liquid	sick
brim	gift	livid	skid
clip	grill	mint	skin
cliff	grim	miss	skip
cling	grin	mist	slim
clink	grip	mix	slip
click	grit	mini	slit
crisps	hill	minicab	snip
chip	him	nib	spill
chicken	his	pig	spilt
children	hit	pill	spin
did	hint	pin	spit
dig	hiss	pick	splint
dim	if	picnic	split
din	ill	pip	stick
dip	in	pit	stiff
disc	it	prick	still
drill	ink	print	sting
drip	kill	quick	stink
drink	king	quilt	strict
dish	kiss	quiz	string
fill	kick	quid	strip
film	kid	rib	swim
flick	kidnap	rid	swing
fling	kit	rig	shin
flip	knit	rip	shrimps
flit	lid	rift	till
fin	lift	ring	tin
Finland	lip	rink	tip

Basic List (contd.)

tick	victim	windmill	whip
trip	visit	wing	whisk
trim	vivid	wink	wring
trick	will	wig	wrist
twig	win	wit	zip
twin	wind	with	

Supplementary

admit	drift	minim	squint
bliss	electric	misfit	stint
brisk	flinch	mishap	swift
clinch	flint	misprint	tilt
critic	inn	ping	timid
disband	inland	sift	twist
disgust	instinct	sin	wisp
dismiss	intact	skill	
distinct	kiln	skimp	
district	kilt	slick	

e

Basic List

bed	exit	mend	spell
beg	exist	mess	spend
bet	expect	metric	spent
bell	expel	nest	stem
belt	extra	net	step
bend	fell	next	swell
bench	felt	neck	seven
contest	French	pen	shelf
credit	flex	pet	tell
cress	get	pelt	ten
crest	help	red	tent
chest	hem	rent	test
chestnut	hen	rest	text
chicken	jet	restless	vest
children	jet lag	sell	web
desk	kept	self	well
dress	left	himself	went
dentist	leg	send	wet
egg	let	sent	west
exam	lend	set	yell
elm	less	slept	yes
electric	men	swept	yet
electronic	melt	smell	

Supplementary

content	extinct	trend	vent
exotic	hectic	trumpet	zest
expand	splendid	upset	

u

Basic List

adult	drug	luck	skull
bud	drum	lunch	slug
bug	drunk	mud	slum
bun	fun	mug	slump
bus	fund	Mum	stump
but	funds	mumps	stub
bulb	fuss	must	stuff
bulk	fluff	munch	suck
bump	gull	nut	sudden
bunk	gum	pub	scrub
blunt	gun	pup	struck
cub	gust	puff	tuck
cuff	gruff	pump	truck
cup	gulp	pulp	trunk
cut	hug	plug	trust
club	hum	plump	up
clump	hump	plus	upset
crust	hut	public	us
crunch	hunt	rub	umbrella
culprit	husband	rug	unless
chestnut	hundred	run	unlock
dud	jug	rung	unpack
dump	jump	rusk	unplug
dust	junk	rust	unstuck
duck	just	rush	unwell
dull	lump	sum	
dusk	lung	sun	

Supplementary

conduct	pun	strung	suspect
disgust	rum	strut	suspend
glut	scum	stun	trump
hub	skulk	stunt	trumpet
hubbub	skunk	subject	tuft
hull	smug	submit	tug
hulk	snub	sulk	unbend
husk	snug	summit	unjust
nun	strum	sump	unrest

49

ck

Basic List

back	kick	picket	stick
black	kick-off	pocket	sticky
block	knock	quack	stock
brick	lack	quick	stockings
bucket	lick	quickly	stuck
click	lock	rock	tack
clock	luck	rocket	tick
cock	lucky	sack	ticket
cricket	mock	sick	track
deck	muck	sock	trick
dock	neck	suck	truck
duck	pack	slack	tuck
duckling	peck	smack	wicket
flick	pick	snack	
flock	pluck	socket	
frock	prick	speck	
jack	packet	stack	
jacket			

Supplementary

attack	hack	reckon	tackle
beckon	heckle	rick	tickle
bracken	hock	sickness	trickle
bracket	locket	slick	tricky
buckle	pickle	smock	wick
cackle	prickle	stickle back	wicked
docket	prickly	stocky	
fickle	racket	stricken	
freckle	reckless	struck	

ee

Basic List

bee	greed	see	screen
beef	greedy	seen	TV screen
bleed	heel	seed	sweet
bleep	indeed	sleep	sweep
creep	jeep	asleep	sheep
deep	keep	sleepless	teens
feed	knee	sleet	tree
feel	kneel	steel	weed
feet	meet	steep	week
fee	need	speed	week-end
free	peep	spree	weep
green	queen	street	wheel

Supplementary

agree	eel	heed	reed
committee	exceed	keel	reel
creed	fleet	keen	screech
creek	freedom	leek	seek
deed	greet	peel	seep
disagree	greetings	proceed	wee

ee - e

freeze	breeze	geese	sleeve
anti-freeze	cheese	Greece	squeeze

eer

beer	commandeer	engineer	queer
career	deer	jeer	sheer
cheer	domineering	peer	volunteer

oo

Basic List

boot	moon	swoop	looked
broom	noon	too	soot
food	proof	toot	took
hoof	roof	troop	wood
hooves	room	zoom	wool
hoop	bedroom	zoomed	cool
loop	root	cook	fool
loot	soon	foot	pool
moo	spoon	good	stool
mood	stoop	look	tool

Supplementary

boom	gloom	roost	hood
bloom	gloomy	scoop	hook
boon	groom	snooze	nook
boost	loom	swoon	rook
booty	loot	brook	woollen
booze	noodles	crook	
doom	poodle	crooked	

oor

floor	moor	poor

oo - e

choose	goose	loose	soothe

Basic List

ar

arm	cardigan	harmless	scarf
alarm	carpet	hard	scarves
arctic	carton	jar	scarlet
are	dark	lard	smart
art	darkness	large	spark
artist	darling	mark	star
bar	dart	marker	start
bark	far	park	tar
barn	farm	parking	tart
car	garden	part	target
card	harm	scar	yard
			sharp

Supplementary

arc	darn	lark	regards
argument	Denmark	marble	remarkable
architect	depart	marmalade	sarcasm
bargain	department	marksman	sarcastic
barman	garlic	margarine	sharpener
carbon	harness	pardon	snarl
cargo	harp	Parliament	startle
carnival	harvest	parsnip	starve
cartoon	jargon	parson	yarn
compartment	larder	regard	

Look the same — sound different

List A

altar	coward	vulgar	apparatus
burglar	custard	regular	particular
cellar	orchard	separate	particularly
collar	vicar	singular	preparation

List B

war	warm	ward
warning	reward	quarter

List C

awkward	backward	towards
afterwards	forward	

Basic List

or

acorn	fort	more	sort
or	forty	morning	stork
cord	forget	or	storm
cork	forgot	platform	stormy
corn	forbid	pork	story
cornet	horse	record	sword
for	horn	recording	torn
form	lord	report	transport
fork	north	sport	

Supplementary

absorb	forbidden	inform	port
afford	ford	morbid	portrait
assorted	forgive	normal	reform
boring	format	northern	resort
carnivorous	formula	orbit	retort
decorate	fortunate	orchard	support
deport	gory	organ	sworn
evaporate	horn	organise	transform
export	humorous	ordinary	vigorously
extort	history	ornament	worn
extraordinary	import	opportunity	
factory	important	performance	

or - e

adore	forecourt	foresight	shore
before	forefinger	forever	sore
bore	forego	horse	store
explore	foreground	ignore	wore
fore	forehead	more	
forearm	foreman	score	
forecast	foresee	snore	

Look the same — sound different

actor	dictator	major	sponsored
bachelor	doctor	memory	tailor
censor	equator	sailor	traitor
collector	junior	senior	visitor
councillor	mayor	sponsor	word

sh

Basic List

ship	shoot	cash	selfish
shop	shark	crash	unselfish
shot	sharp	clash	finish
shut	sharpen	flash	punish
shed	short	mash	punishment
shell	shrimp	rash	vanish
shelf	shrink	smash	wish
shock	shampoo	splash	posh
sheet	she	dish	hush
sheep	ash	fish	rush

Supplementary

shift	shunt	flesh	slush
shin	bash	flush	tarnish
shred	blush	gash	trash
shrill	brandish	harsh	
shrub	brash	lash	
shrug	diminish	mesh	

ch

Basic List

chat	cheek	munch
chap	chicken	punch
chin	check	bench
chip	cherry	clench
chips	chess	French
chill	chestnut	arch
chilled	much	march
chop	such	speech
chest	lunch	which
chum	bunch	
chunk	crunch	

Supplementary

channel	cheque	clinch
char	chimpanzee	orchard
charge	chink	parched
charm	chit	parchment
chart	chuck	
charity	brunch	

ch = k

school	chloride	chrysanthemum
ache	chlorine	stomach
headache	choral	scheme
Christ	choir -	technical
Christmas	*pronounced Welsh*	technician
Christopher	*way — k-oir*	technique
Christine	chord	technology
christen	chorister	technological
christening	choreographer	scholarship
chaos	chrome	architect
chaotic	chromium	archives
character	chronic	orchestra
chemical	chronicle	orchid
chemist	chronological	
chemistry	chrysalis	

56

tch

catch	satchel	ditch
match	snatch	kitchen
hatch	scratch	pitch
batch	fetch	switch
latch	ketchup	witch
patch	stretch	

ch = sh

champagne	chef	chute
charade	chic	panache
chamois	chivalry	parachute
chauffeur	chivalrous	brochure

th

Basic List

thank	thick	with
thin	three	within
thing	cloth	maths
think	moth	method
theft	froth	arithmetic
thud	the	fifth
thump	than	sixth
thrush	that	seventh
thrash	them	tenth
thrill	themselves	eleventh
thrilling	then	length
throb	this	

Supplementary

therapist	thrust	lengthy
therapy	thug	lethargic
thrift	anthem	mathematics
thrifty	anthology	

Basic List   **a-e**

blame	grape	salesman
blaze	grapes	salesmen
blade	grade	same
brave	gape	save
ape	hate	scale
awake	lame	scrape
cake	lane	shade
came	late	shame
cane	made	shake
case	make	shave
cave	make-up	shape
chase	male	skate
craze	female	slate
date	mate	snake
daze	name	spade
fade	nickname	take
fame	pane	tame
flame	pavement	taste
flames	plane	tape
frame	plate	trade
flake	safe	tradesman
cornflakes	safely	wade
game	safety	waste
gale	safety belt	wake
gate	safety pin	
gave	sale	

ace

ace	brace	menace
face	bracelet	misplace
place	deface	pace
palace	disgrace	trace
race	grace	
space	lace	

age

age	page	wages
cage	stage	engage
change	wage	engaged

damage	postage	salvage
image	rage	stage
manage	rampage	usage
message		

Supplementary

ale	inflame	persuaded
amaze	intake	quake
base	invade	range
based	lathe	rave
basement	maple	sake
behave	membrane	sane
cape	misbehave	stale
dame	mistake	stake
evade	mundane	strange
exchange	octave	upgrade
glaze	octane	whale
grave	parade	Wales
graze	pave	
haste	persuade	

ate

ate	exaggerate	private
date	excavate	rate
accommodate	fate	rates
animate	fortunate	rebate
animated	fortunately	renovate
chocolate	grate	rotate
debate	grateful	senate
desperate	illustrate	separate
dilapidated	immediate	state
dominate	immediately	statesman
donate	inflate	stimulate
educate	inmate	stipulate
emigrate	irrigate	simulate
estate	irritate	update
estate agent	isolate	ultimate
estimate	migrate	vacate
evaporate	penetrate	
evaporated	populate	

i-e

Basic List

bike	miles	stripe
bite	mine	swipe
bride	nine	spike
bridegroom	nineteen	time
chime	ninety	tide
crime	pile	tile
drive	pine	tribe
arrive	pipe	unite
five	prize	wide
fine	pride	wife
glide	quite	wine
hike	revise	wipe
hive	ride	while
hide	ripe	whine
divide	side	white
inside	beside	wise
invite	site	write
knife	size	die
life	smile	died
line	shine	lie
like	slide	lied
dislike	spine	pie
lime	stride	tie
mile	strike	tied

ice

ice	price	twice
mice	slice	vice
nice	sliced	advice
rice	spice	device

ire

fire	desire	require
hire	entire	required
wire	enquire	spire
admire	expire	tire
acquire	inspire	tired
aspire	retire	umpire
conspire	retired	Ireland

Supplementary

advise	excitement	recognise
advertise	extradite	revive
advertisement	file	shrine
arise	crocodile	slime
aside	grime	snide
decide	incline	spite
define	jibe	spiteful
definite	mime	sprite
definitely	pantomime	strife
defile	oblige	strive
deprive	organise	subside
deride	parasite	subscribe
describe	polite	subsidize
despite	prescribe	swine
dime	preside	thrive
dine	prime	tripe
excite	provide	

Change 'y' to 'i' and add 'ed'

ally - allied	dry - dried	satisfy - satisfied
apply - applied	fry - fried	try - tried
cry - cried	rely - relied	
deny - denied	reply - replied	

Look the same — sound different

police	magazine	machine

o-e

Basic List

alone	hose	stone
bone	hotel	stole
broke	joke	stove
choke	nose	stroke
chose	note	those
close	lonely	tone
closed	loneliness	vote
clothes	motel	wrote
coke	phone	whole
cone	telephone	woke
dole	pole	zone
dose	poke	toe
doze	Pope	toes
drove	robe	foe
hole	rope	hoe
home	rose	roe
homeless	scone	oboe
hope	slope	tomatoes
hoped	smoke	potatoes
hopeless	spoke	

Supplementary

compose	globe	probe
depose	grope	prose
disclose	impose	quote
dispose	mole	revoke
dope	ode	role
episode	poem	scope
erode	poet	sole
explode	pole	stoke
expose	pose	

Look the same — sound different

gone	does	shoe

u-e

Basic List

cube	nude	clue
flute	prune	glue
fume	rude	true
fumes	rule	cue
June	tune	due
huge	tube	argue
include	salute	queue
mule	blue	
mute	Tuesday	

use

use	amuse	refuse
used	fuse	
excuse	accuse	

Supplementary

accrue	dune	reduce
acute	ensue	refute
capsule	exclude	subdue
commune	execute	substitute
compute	exude	truce
consume	issue	cruel
continue	obtuse	cruet
continued	presume	duel
crude	puce	duet
dispute	pursue	fluent
disuse	rebuke	fuel
disused	recluse	gruelling

ure

assure	insure	posture
capture	leisure	procure
cure	lecture	pure
departure	lecturer	secure
ensure	literature	sure
failure	lure	unsure
figure	manure	temperature
immature	mature	venture
impure	pressure	vulture
injure	picture	

e-e

these	complete	scene
extreme	completely	
extremely	theme	

ai

Basic List

rain	aim	maize
train	bargain	mountain
drain	chain	nail
raid	claim	paid
rail	complain	paint
sail	daily	plaice
snail	daisy	plain
tail	explain	remain
pain	fail	saint
painful	frail	Spain
painless	faint	sprain
wait	gain	stain
waiting	grain	strain
waited	hail	trail
afraid	jail	training
again	mail	waist
against	maid	
aid	main	

Supplementary

acquainted	disclaim	raisin
ailing	entail	reclaim
ailment	faith	refrain
bail	maiden	regain
bailiff	maim	restrain
bait	maintain	retail
braid	maisonette	retain
Braille	obtain	staid
braise	plaintiff	strait
captain	portrait	tainted
complaint	praise	unaided
contain	prevail	unfaithful
dainty	quaint	vain
detail	raise	waive
detain		

air

air	fairy	lair
affair	flair	pair
chair	hair	repair
chairman	hairy	prairie
dairy	impair	stair
fair	impaired	upstairs

oa

Basic List

boat	goat	roam
coast	groan	roast
coat	load	soak
coach	loaded	soaked
coal	loaf	soaking
coal-mine	moan	soap
cloak	moaning	stoat
cloakroom	moat	throat
cocoa	oak	toad
float	oats	toadstool
foam	poach	toast
goal	road	

Supplementary

approach	gloat	loathe
approached	goad	oath
bloated	hoax	reproach
coax	load	shoal
foal	loam	

oar

boar	coarse	hoarse
board	hoard	roar
cupboard	hoarding	soar

Sounds the same — Looks different

broad   abroad

ir

Basic List

bird	fir (tree)	squirt
birth	firm	squirted
birthday	first	thirst
birch	flirt	thirsty
circus	girl	thirty
circle	sir	thirteen
chirp	skirt	third
dirt	shirt	
dirty	stir	

Supplementary

birthrate	girth	virtue
circuit	mirth	virtuoso
circular	shirk	virtuous
circulate	skirmish	whirl
circumstances	squirm	whirlpool
confirm	twirl	
girdle	virtual	

ou

Basic List

about	around	outfit
aloud	shout	outing
cloud	shouting	pouch
count	shouted	pounce
found	sound	proud
ground	amount	scout
house	blouse	south
loud	bounce	spout
mouse	couch	sprout
mouth	county	stout
out	foul	thousand
outside	hound	trout
pound	lounge	without
round	mountain	wound

Supplementary

account	flounce	resound
accountant	foundry	rouse
announce	fountain	scoundrel
bound	gout	surround
boundary	grouse	surrounded
council	lout	slouch
councillor	mound	vouch
countless	noun	our
crouch	oust	flour
discount	pout	hour
doubt	recount	sour
doubtful	rehouse	
doubtless	renounce	

ea (ee)

Basic List

beach	jeans	seaside
bead	leaf	seat
beak	leaves	speak
bean	leak	steal
beat	meal	steam
cheap	mean	steaming
cheat	meat	stream
clean	pea	tea
cream	peas	teaspoon
dream	peach	teach
each	peaches	team
eat	peanut	treacle
east	please	treat
easy	pleased	treatment
flea	read	weak
heat	sea	
heating	season	

Supplementary

beacon	feasibility	sheaf
beam	freak	sleazy
bleak	grease	sneak
beast	greasy	streak
breach	ideal	teak
cease	lead	tease
ceaseless	leading	teat
creak	league	treason
crease	lean	treaty
creature	leap	unbeaten
deal	lease	veal
defeat	least	wean
eagle	leave	weave
ease	meagre	wheat
easily	meaning	wreath
eaves	meantime	yeast
eavesdrop	peace	zeal
feast	seal	
feasible	seam	

ear

appear	ear	spear
beard	fear	tear
bleary	gear	tearful
clear	hear	weary
clearly	near	wearily
dear	nearly	year
dreary	rear	
disappear	shears	

Look the same — sound different

(a)

earn	early	pearl
earnings	heard	search
earth	learn	yearn

(b)

bear	pear	wear
bearable	swear	
unbearable	tear	

(c)

heart	heartless	hearth
hearty		

ea-e

breathe	grease	peaceful
cease	heave	please
crease	increase	tease
decrease	lease	weave
disease	leave	
ease	peace	

ay

Basic List

day	bay	played
today	clay	playing
holiday	crayon	railway
Sunday	delay	ray
Monday	display	say
Tuesday	hay	stay
Wednesday	lay	stray
Thursday	may	tray
Friday	May	way
Saturday	pay	
away	play	

Supplementary

ashtray	fray	repayment
astray	layman	slay
bayonet	Norway	spray
bray	pray	sway
decay	relay	X-ray
defray	repay	

ur

Basic List

burn	fur (coat)	surname
burning	furnish	surgeon
burnt	further	surprise
burglar	hurt	surprised
burst	murder	Saturday
church	nurse	Thursday
churn	purple	turban
curl	purr	turkey
curly	purse	turn
curtain	suburb	turnip
disturb	surf	turnstile
disturbed	surface	urgent

Supplementary

absurd	hurl	surly
blurb	hurtle	surmise
burden	lurk	surmount
burgle	murmur	surplus
burly	murky	survey
bursar	occur	survive
churlish	occurred	turbine
curb	purchase	turf
curse	purge	turntable
curt	purl	turpentine
curtail	purpose	Turkey
curve	pursue	urban
furnace	slur	urchin
furniture	spur	urge
furthest	sturdy	urgency
furtive	surcharge	urn
gurgle	surge	
hurdle	surgical	

Look the same — sound different

bury   burial

aw

Basic List

awful	hawk	sawdust
awkward	hawthorn	shawl
bawl	jaw	straw
claw	law	strawberry
crawl	lawful	sprawl
crawled	unlawful	sprawled
dawn	lawn	sprawling
dawdle	paw	thaw
draw	prawn	yawn
drawn	raw	yawned
drawer	saw	

Supplementary

awe	caw	pawn
awning	drawl	tawny
brawl	flaw	withdraw
brawn	lawyer	

oi

Basic List

avoid	noisy	disappointment
boil	noiseless	poison
choice	oil	soil
coin	ointment	spoil
foil	point	spoilt
join	appoint	spoiled
joint	disappoint	toilet
noise	disappointed	voice

Supplementary

broiler	jointly	moisture
coil	joist	poise
exploit	loin	quoits
groin	loiter	toil
hoist	moist	void

er

Basic List

anger	murdered	silver
barber	never	sister
beaker	nerve	spider
better	number	summer
clever	order	supper
danger	ordered	sup̲ermarket
different	offer	swerve
dinner	operate	swerved
driver	over	term
energy	paper	thunder
ever	partner	thundered
every	passenger	transfer
exercise	pepper	under
germ	perfect	underground
her	perhaps	understand
herself	permit	understood
interest	person	yesterday
interesting	proper	winter
kerb	remember	whisper
jersey	remembered	whispered
letter	river	September
matter	runner	October
member	serve	November
meter	service	December
modern	sharpener	
murder	shepherd	

Supplementary

amber	exaggerate	monastery
adverb	fertilizer	numerous
advert	fiery	observe
advertisement	geranium	observant
anniversary	Germany	opera
average	germinate	otter
boomerang	girder	persuade
border	herb	reserve
certain	herd	reservoir
certainly	interrupt	refer
character	jerk	referee
circumference	Jersey	reference
concern	jeweller	stationer
considerable	jewellery	stationery
customer	later	superb
dagger	lecturer	supersonic
deliver	lever	supervise
delivery	liberty	Switzerland
desperate	Mediterranean	temperature
diverge	meter	terminal
divert	mineral	thermometer
emergency	Minister	

all/al

Basic List

all	stalls	almost
ball	tall	already
football	wall	altogether
call	talk	always
fall	talking	halt
hall	walk	salt
small	walking	
stall	chalk	

Supplementary

pitfall	altered	stalk
recall	bald	walnut
recalled	false	walrus
squall	falter	waltz
wallpaper	malt	
alter	scald	

al ending

arrival	final	punctual
annual	fatal	principal
capital	formal	original
carnival	industrial	removal
cathedral	local	several
central	mammal	terminal
choral	material	trial
criminal	musical	usual
cymbal	natural	usually
equal	national	
festival	professional	

cial

social	especially	essential
special	financial	

ea (ĕ)

Basic List

bread	headmistress	already
breakfast	heavy	spread
breath	health	sweat
breathless	healthy	threat
dead	instead	threaten
death	lead	treasure
deaf	leather	wealth
dread	meant	wealthy
dreadful	pleasant	weather
head	unpleasant	weapon
headache	read	
ahead	ready	

Supplementary

breadth	heavily	readily
breast	jealous	steady
breathalize	measure	steadily
cleanliness	peasant	thread
heather	pleasure	tread
heaven	Reading	treasury

Look the same — sound different

break	great	steak

ow (cow)

Basic List

bow	down	how
brown	drown	now
clown	drowsy	owl
cow	flower	row
crown	flowered	tower
crowd	frown	town
crowded	frowned	

Supplementary

allow	gown	prowler
brow	growl	renown
eyebrow	growled	rowdy
browse	however	scowl
coward	howl	scowled
cower	howled	shower
cowered	howler	sow
chow	power	towel
dowry	powerful	trowel
endow	power point	vow
endowed	powder	vowed
fowl	prow	vowel
glower	prowl	

igh

Basic List

bright	frightened	tonight
delight	high	right
delighted	knight	sigh
delightful	light	sighed
fight	lighting	sight
fighting	lightning	tight
flight	might	tights
fright	night	
frighten	midnight	

Supplementary

alight	mighty	slight
blight	plight	thigh
frightful	eyesight	twilight

a (ar)

Basic List

after	danced	master
ask	dancing	headmaster
asked	dancer	mask
asking	drama	nasty
basket	fast	pass
bath	fasten	passing
bathroom	unfasten	passed
blast	(zip) fastener	passport
branch	father	path
branches	gasp	plant
brass	glass	plaster
can't	grandma	rather
class	grass	staff
daft	grasp	underpass
dance	last	

Supplementary

advance	flask	rafter
advantage	France	ranch
aghast	gala	rascal
bask	glance	rasp
cast	graft	raspberry
chance	grant	saga
chant	lance	shaft
clasp	mast	slander
command	overcast	slant
commander	overdraft	task
craft	pastoral	trance
aircraft	pasture	vantage
craftsman	plasterer	vase
demand	prance	vast
disaster	raft	

Sound the same — look different

calf	calm	qualm
half	palm	

o (ŭ)

Basic List

brother	other	become
cover	otherwise	becoming
covered	another	done
discover	oven	dove
discovered	son	glove
dozen	won	love
front	wonder	loving
London	wondered	money
Monday	wonderful	monkey
month	worry	none
monthly	above	some
mother	come	sponge

Supplementary

accompany	government	shovel
company	honey	stomach
frontier	onion	ton
govern	shove	tongue

Related words

one   once

y (ī)

Basic List

by	frying	sky
cry	goodbye	spy
cycle	my	shy
bicycle	myself	try
tricycle	multiply	trying
dry	nylon	why
fly	pylon	
fry	reply	

Supplementary

ally	occupy	style
apply	ply	styling
awry	plywood	stylist
comply	pry	spry
defy	python	thyme
deny	rely	thyroid
dye	rhyme	tycoon
hyacinth	rye	typist
hydrant	sly	tyrant
hydrofoil	sty	wry

y (ĭ)

mystery	lyrics	systematic
mysterious	physics	syllable
crystal	physical	syllabus
crypt	pyjamas	symptom
cymbals	pyramid	syrup
Egypt	rhythm	syringe
gym	sycamore	tyrannical
gymnasium	sympathy	typical
gymnast	sympathetic	
hymn	system	

ow (ō)

Basic List

arrow	growing	owner
below	grown	pillow
blow	hollow	row
borrow	know	show
bow	(knowledge)	slow
bowled	low	slowly
bowler	marrow	snow
crow	meadow	snowing
elbow	mow	snowed
follow	mower	throw
followed	narrow	tomorrow
glow	owe	yellow
grow	own	window

Supplementary

barrow	lowly	sow
bellows	mellow	stow
disown	minnow	tow
fellow	sallow	widow
flow	shallow	willow
growth	sorrow	
lower	sorrowful	

ew

Basic List

blew	flew	news
chew	grew	newspaper
chewing	jewel	nephew
crew	jeweller	screw
dew	jewellery	stew
drew	knew	threw
few	new	

Supplementary

brew	pewter	stewardess
brewery	review	view
ewe	shrew	views
Jew	shrewd	yew
Jewish	skewer	
pew	steward	

oy

Basic List

annoy	employment	joy
annoyed	unemployment	loyal
boy	employee	disloyal
destroy	employer	royal
destroyed	enjoy	royalty
employ	enjoyed	toy
employed	enjoyment	

Supplementary

alloy	convoy	ploy
boycott	coy	soya
buoy	destroyer	voyage
buoyant	foyer	
cloy	oyster	

au

Basic List

astronaut	autumn	haunted
August	cause	laundry
auburn	caused	sauce
audience	fault	saucy
author	faulty	saucepan
automatic	haunt	saucer

Supplementary

auction	automobile	gaunt
audacity	Automobile	gauze
audible	Association	haul
audit	auxiliary	haulage
audition	caustic	launch
auditorium	cauterize	maul
augment	caution	staunch
augur	clause	trauma
aura	daub	traumatic
authentic	daunted	undaunted
authoritarian	faultless	vault
authority	fauna	vaunt
Local Authority	flaunt	
authorize	gaudy	

Look the same — sound different

Australia	cauliflower	sausages
Austria	claustrophobia	
because	sausage	

augh

| daughter | haughty | slaughter |
| fraught | naughty | |

Look the same — sound different

| draught | laughter |
| laugh | laughing |

ī

Basic List

behind	diamond	lion
blind	diary	lioness
find	final	minor
kind	finally	minus
kindness	finalist	pirate
unkind	finance	primary
mind	hijack	private
pint	hijacker	remind
wind	hijacked	silent
child	hibernate	silence
mild	hibernation	sign
wild	iron	signpost
Bible	island	tidy
bicycle	ideal	tiger
tricycle	identical	tiny
climb	liar	trifle
diagonal	library	triangle
diagram	lido	violin
dial	lilac	

Supplementary

biology	isolation	rind
crisis	ivory	rival
dialect	ivy	siren
diameter	liable	tidily
divert	liability	violet
entitled	libel	via
grind	librarian	viable
identify	microscope	vibration
idle	migraine	viper
irate	migrate	violent
iris	pioneer	vital
isolate	primus	wily

ou (ŭ)

Basic List

country	double	touch
courage	flourish	touched
discourage	flourishing	trouble
encourage	nourish	young
couple	nourishing	youngest
coupling	southern	younger

Look the same — sound different

group	youth	mouldy
coupon	shoulder	smoulder
soup	poultry	moult
wound	mould	

a (ŏ)

Basic List

squash	what	squat
swallow	whatever	squatter
swan	yacht	swab
swap	blancmange	swamp
wand	quads	swamped
want	quadrangle	swastika
wanted	quality	swat
was	quantity	waffle
wasn't	quarrel	wander
wash	quarry	wandered
washing	squabble	wandering
wasp	squabbling	watched
watch	squadron	watching

Supplementary

quad	quality	squander
quadruple	qualm	wad
quadruplet	quarantine	waft
quagmire	squad	wan
qualification	squalid	wanton
qualified	squalor	watt

ough

Basic List

bought	nought	thoughtless
brought	ought	thoughtful
fought	thought	

Look the same — sound different

(a)

| bough | plough | ploughing |
| drought | ploughed | |

(b)

| though | although | dough |

(c)

| enough | rough | tough |

(d)

| cough | trough |

(e)

| through | throughout |

(f)

| borough | thorough | thoroughly |

ph

Basic List

phone	atmosphere	pamphlet
telephone	biography	paragraph
phoned	autobiography	phantom
phoning	emphasis	phase
photo	emphasize	phrase
photograph	emphatic	pheasant
photocopy	geography	physical
photocopier	graph	physics
photostat	hemisphere	sophisticated
elephant	hyphen	sphere
nephew	microphone	triumph
Philip	nymph	triumphant
alphabet	orphan	trophy
autograph	orphanage	xylophone

Supplementary

blaspheme	philanthropist	physiology
blasphemous	philatelist	physiotherapy
blasphemy	phial	physique
catastrophe	philosopher	prophecy
catastrophic	philosophical	prophet
decipher	phlegm	sapphire
emphatically	phoenix	siphon
epitaph	phobia	spherical
euphoria	phonetics	sphinx
euphemism	phosphate	stratosphere
paraphernalia	phosphorus	telegraph
pharmacist	photogenic	telephonist
phenomena	physician	
philanthropic	physicist	

o

Basic List

go	moment	poster
ago	most	polo
no	mostly	potato
nowhere	micro	programme
no-one	microphone	robot
nobody	microchip	Roman
bonus	motor	total
brochure	motorist	won't
both	motor vehicle	zero
cocoa	motion	bold
coconut	notice	cold
crocus	obey	fold
donate	only	gold
donation	over	hold
don't	polar	old
echo	polite	older
ghost	police	oldest
going	post	sold
host	postage	told
local	postpone	wold

Supplementary

alto	motivate	progress
Anglo	motivation	prohibit
aroma	notion	prolong
bogus	nobility	protest
chromium	notification	provide
crony	notify	quota
docile	obedient	quotation
ego	occasion	quotient
embargo	occasionally	robust
extrovert	odious	rogue
focal	omit	romance
focus	omit	romantic
fro	omission	rondo
global	onus	rosary
gross	opus	rota
grotesque	opium	rotation
holy	overture	rotary
kimono	ozone	slogan
locate	poky	sofa
location	polio	solar
locust	posy	yoga
locomotive	probation	zodiac
lotion	profile	

are (air)

Basic List

aware	fare	scared
bare	flare	scarecrow
beware	glare	share
blare	hare	snare
care	mare	spare
careful	parents	square
careless	grandparents	stare
caretaker	rare	stared
dare	scare	

Supplementary

compare	prepare	transparent
compared	rarely	wares
declare	scarce	warehouse
farewell	scarcely	

ie/ei

Basic List

brief	piece	besiege
belief	mantelpiece	priest
believe	relief	field
chief	relieve	shield
handkerchief	shriek	yield
grief	thief	fierce
grieve	thieves	pierce
mischief	achieve	piercing
mischievous	achievement	
niece	siege	

i before e except after c

receive	conceited	deceit
ceiling	conceive	deceitful
conceit	misconceive	deceive

but

leisure	foreign	foreigner

Silent Letters

w

wrap	wrestling	wrong
wreck	write	answer
wreckage	written	sword
wrestler	wrote	

u

build	guessed	guaranteed
builder	guest	guarantor
building	guide	guerrilla
built	guided	tongue
biscuit	guard	vague
disguise	guilty	vogue
guess	guarantee	

kn

knee	knit	knocker
kneel	knitted	knocked
knelt	knitting	knot
knife	knob	know
knives	knock	knew

t

castle	fastener	often
fasten	listen	thistle
unfasten	listened	whistle
fastened	listener	

gn

gnat	gnaw	sign
gnarled	gnome	design

n

autumn	column	hymn
condemn		

d

budget   midget

sc

scene   scientist   muscle
scenery   scientific   fascinate
scent   scissors   schedule
science

b

bomb   crumb   numb
bomber   dumb   plumber
comb   lamb

Soft c (followed by 'e', 'i' or 'y')

accent	criticism	proceed
access	decide	process
accept	decision	receive
accelerate	excite	recent
accident	medicine	recently
circle	notice	success
circus	noticeably	succeed
circumference	office	
circumstances	practice	

ci (sh)

conscience	technician	special
electrician	musician	concerto
especially	magician	

Soft g (followed by 'e', 'i' or 'y')

age	George	giant
damage	Georgina	gigantic
garage	geography	gipsy
manage	generation	imagine
manageable	generosity	imagination
message	huge	magic
messenger	knowledge	religion
postage	knowledgeable	engine
rage	privilege	engineer
rampage	sergeant	gym
salvage	tragedy	gymnasium
exaggerate	vegetable	energy

tion

Basic List

station	organisation	interruption
alteration	preparation	production
accommodation	punctuation	question
association	action	repetition
conversation	condition	section
education	correction	attention
examination	description	invention
invitation	direction	mention
respiration	exception	objection
separation	exhibition	
situation	fraction	

ous

disastrous	nervous	deciduous
famous	numerous	porous
humorous	ridiculous	vigorous
jealous	carnivorous	
marvellous	coniferous	

ious

curious	mysterious	obviously
envious	previous	
industrious	serious	

cious

atrocious	precious	anxious
conscious	spacious	conscientious
unconscious	suspicious	

our

armour	flavour	labour
behaviour	harbour	neighbour
colour	honour	rumour
favour	honourable	vapour
favourite	humour	

Look the same — sound different

(a)

| journey | journal | journalist |

(b)

| tour | tourist |

(c)

| your | course | court |

sion

Basic List

admission	professional	invasion
discussion	confusion	occasion
mission	decision	pension
permission	division	provision
possession	erosion	vision
procession	excursion	television
profession	explosion	

ary

Basic List

January	necessary	extraordinary
February	stationary	voluntary
complimentary	supplementary	Hungary
contemporary	temporary	
library	ordinary	

able

Basic List

vegetable	disagreeable	knowledgeable
miserable	comparable	reasonable
available	considerable	unreasonable
agreeable	manageable	

ance

Basic List

balance	performance	extravagance
entrance	acquaintance	ignorance
nuisance	appearance	insurance
distance	alliance	substance
attendance	assistance	circumstances

ant

Basic List

brilliant	elegant	sergeant
distant	extravagant	vacant
elephant	ignorant	

ent

Basic List

absent	excitement	intelligent
argument	commencement	obedient
accompaniment	experiment	Parliament
announcement	efficient	persistent
apparent	magnificent	prominent
compliment	inconvenient	resident
development	ingredient	sufficient
dependent	independent	
different	innocent	

ence

Basic List

absence	sentence	intelligence
difference	reference	obedience
commence	conscience	
convenience	experience	

le

Basic List

angle	pebble	sensible
Bible	possible	simple
doodle	principle	single
example	probable	trifle
horrible	raffle	uncle
idle	responsible	visible
jungle	sample	invisible
miracle	scramble	
muscle	scribble	

ful

Basic List

artful	hopeful	truthful
beautiful	painful	wasteful
delightful	peaceful	wilful
fulfil	skilful	wonderful
grateful	successful	
helpful	thoughtful	

fully

Basic List

beautifully	successfully	wonderfully
hopefully	truthfully	

ly

Basic List

equally	elderly	particularly
especially	excitedly	probably
finally	immediately	quietly
gradually	noisily	truly
naturally	noticeably	voluntarily
really	sparsely	wholly
usually	family	
definitely	obviously	

Double consonant/short vowel

Basic List

address	difficult	raffle
attic	exaggerate	rubbish
accommodation	embarrass	recommend
beginning	fitted	slipped
bitter	filled	success
brilliant	foggy	suggest
butterfly	happen	scribble
collect	hidden	summit
collection	luggage	traffic
curriculum	mammal	tunnel
recollect	narrate	valley
committee	narrative	winner
dagger	passage	winning
dinner	passenger	

Alphabetical Index

ă	44	ea (ĕ) dictation	18
ă dictation	9	ea-e	70
a (ar)	80	ear	70
a (ar) dictation	20	e-e	64
a (ŏ)	87	ee	51
a (ŏ) dictation	24	ee dictation	10
able	99	ee-e	51
able dictation	33	eer	51
a-e	58	ei	93
a-e dictation	12	ei dictation	28
ai	64	ence	100
ai dictation	14	ence dictation	39
air	65	ent	100
all/al	76	er	74
all/al dictation	18	er dictation	18
ance	99	ew	84
ance dictation	34	ew dictation	22
ant	99	fully	101
ant dictation	34	fully dictation	37
ar	53	gn	94
ar dictation	10	gn dictation	29
are (air)	92	ĭ	46
are (air) dictation	26	ĭ dictation	9
ary	99	ī	86
ary dictation	32	ī dictation	24
au	85	ice	60
au dictation	24	ie	93
aw	73	ie dictation	28
aw dictation	16	i-e	60
ay	71	i-e dictation	12
ay dictation	16	igh	79
b (silent)	95	igh dictation	20
c (soft)	96	ir	67
c (soft) dictation	31	ir dictation	14
ch	56	ire	61
ch dictation	10	kn	94
ch (k)	56	kn dictation	29
ch (k) dictation	28	ly	101
ch (sh)	57	ly dictation	37
cial	76	n (silent)	94
ci (sh)	96	n (silent) dictation	30
ci dictation	36	ŏ	45
cious	97	ŏ dictation	9
cious dictation	36	ō	90
ck	50	ō dictation	26
ck dictation	9	o (ŭ)	81
d (silent)	95	o (ŭ) dictation	20
double consonant/short vowel	102	oa	66
double consonant/short vowel dictation	39	oa dictation	14
ĕ	48	oar	66
ĕ dictation	9	o-e	62
ea (ee)	69	o-e dictation	12
ea (ee) dictation	16	oi	73
ea (ĕ)	77	oi dictation	18
		oo	52

103

oo dictation	10	sh dictation	9
oo-e	52	sion	98
oo-e dictation	10	sion dictation	36
oor	52	t (silent)	94
or	54	t (silent) dictation	29
or dictation	10	tch	57
or-e	54	th	57
ou ($\breve{u}$)	87	th dictation	9
ou ($\breve{u}$) dictation	24	tion	97
ou (out)	68	tion dictation	32
ou (out) dictation	14	$\breve{u}$	49
ough	88	$\breve{u}$ dictation	9
ough dictation	26	u (silent)	94
ous	97	u (silent) dictation	29
ous dictation	36	u-e	63
our	98	u-e dictation	12
our dictation	37	ur	72
ow ($\bar{o}$)	83	ur dictation	16
ow ($\bar{o}$) dictation	22	ure	64
ow (cow)	78	use	63
ow (cow) dictation	20	w (silent)	94
oy	84	w (silent) dictation	29
oy dictation	22	war	53
ph	89	y (ee)	11
ph dictation	26	y ($\bar{i}$)	82
sc	95	y ($\bar{i}$) dictation	22
sc dictation	29	y ($\breve{i}$)	82
sh	55	y ($\breve{i}$) dictation	28